WHAT DID JESUS SAY?

WHAT DID JESUS SAY?

WILLIAM S. EPPS

A DAILY DEVOTIONAL JOURNAL

JUDSON PRESS ★ VALLEY FORGE

WHAT DID JESUS SAY? A Daily Devotional Journal

Unless otherwise specified, Scripture verses are based on the King James Version (KJV), although the author frequently paraphrases the KJV to make Jesus' words reflect modern conversational style.

When specified, Bible quotations marked CEV are from the Contemporary English Version. Copyright © 1991, 1992, 1995 by American Bible Society. Used by permission. Bible quotations marked NLT are from the *Holy Bible,* New Living Translation, copyright © 1996. Used by permission of Tyndale House Publishers, Inc., Wheaton, IL 60189. All rights reserved. Bible quotations marked NRSV are from the New Revised Standard Version of the Bible, copyright © 1989 by the Division of Christian Education of the National Council of the Churches of Christ in the United States of America. Used by permission. All rights reserved.

Printed in the U.S.A.

This devotional journal is dedicated to
God, Jesus, and the Holy Spirit
for making life possible.

And to my parents,
Charles T. Epps Sr. and Pauline Jacqueline Epps,
who nurtured me in the Christian faith.

To my brother and sister,
Charles T. Epps Jr. and Paula P. Johnson,
who provided opportunity for me to practice the Christian faith.

To my family,
Agretta Denise, Jacqueline Jeannelle, and Andrea Nichole,
who provide opportunity for me to develop in the Christian faith.

And to Second Baptist Church of Los Angeles,
California, where I am privileged to pastor.
This community provides the opportunity for me
to mature in the Christian faith.

ACKNOWLEDGMENTS

I WOULD BE REMISS IF I DID NOT ACKNOWLEDGE THOSE WHO WERE instrumental to this publication. First, I am indebted to Dr. Gardner C. Taylor, who interceded on my behalf with Judson Press. And I am indebted to Dr. David Scholer, Dean at Fuller Theological Seminary and an editorial advisor to Judson Press, for requesting consideration of my work. Neither had to do what they did, and I am grateful.

I am indebted to Dera Tatum, who serves as the editor of all of my printed material. I am beholden to my staff for creating the necessary space so that I could complete this work. I am particularly grateful to Gerald Adams, who serves as my administrative assistant and general all-around person who handles whatever I need him to handle.

Also, I am thankful for Greg Morris, who serves as my assistant, for his imaginative suggestions. Moreover, I am appreciative of Mildred Lovett, director of our child-care facility, for her constant encouragement with regard to the benefits of such a journal as this.

Finally, I am indebted to the congregation I pastor for the privilege to do something like this for them each year. I have grown immeasurably as a result of their acceptance, and I give to them each year a through-the-Bible journal to facilitate their spiritual growth and maturity.

No pastor could wish for a more caring and encouraging congregation than what I have been given in Second Baptist. I am also appreciative for my extended family, the Joneses—Harvey, Billie and Sonja—for their constant encouragement and to Jini Kilgore for proofreading this publication.

Finally, I owe a debt of gratitude to Judson Press—their acquisitions editor, Randy Frame, and associate publisher Linda Peavy—for guiding me through the process of becoming an author.

INTRODUCTION

OF ALL OF THE MEMORABLE VERSES OF SCRIPTURE IN SACRED WRIT, no words are more precious and priceless than those spoken by Jesus, our Savior. With that in mind, it seems appropriate that a daily, inspirational devotional that shares a word from Jesus is a great way to encourage, challenge, or begin or complete each day.

In the following pages are words from the One who is known as the Prince of Peace. They are precious because of who said them, and they are priceless because of their worth. They speak to the quintessential condition of human existence with the kind of clarity that provides unmistakable direction. Ask yourself as you face your day what Jesus would say.

In order to maximize the intended benefit of this inspirational journal, it may help you to refer to the entire passage from which the quote is taken. This will enable you to grasp the context of the words of Jesus for the day.

I encourage you to meditate on the closing thought or question for the day. Don't just read it and move on. Allow God to speak to your spirit about how Jesus' words can instruct and encourage you thousands of years after he spoke them.

Finally, write about how you can apply the words of Jesus to your life, focusing on your spiritual growth. Please do not let the words of Jesus lie flat in your life. Instead, respond by appropriating his words for your life and for the growth of your faith.

JANUARY 1 🌿
NEW YEAR'S DAY

How is it that you sought me? (Luke 2:49)

Uncertainty causes anxiety that robs us of life's joy. We seek and search in order to find what we need to give us peace of mind. Take a moment as you begin the year to chart a course that will draw you near to the Lord and to the Lord's precious words, words that provide clear direction for our lives.

How will you replace your uncertainty with the Lord's certainty so that you can move from anxiety to assurance?

_____

_____

_____

_____

_____

_____

_____

_____

_____

_____

_____

Did you not know that I must be about my Father's business?
(Luke 2:49)

What are you doing with your life? Are you wasting time? Creating strife? Making of your existence something you do not like? Or do you know beyond a shadow of a doubt exactly where your life is heading? The compelling interest of Jesus' life was to be a part of activity in which God was involved. Make up your mind as you begin this year to build a life that will draw you near to the source of life.

As you consider how your energy and time are both consumed, what do you need to do to develop a God-centered life?

_____

_____

_____

_____

_____

_____

_____

_____

_____

_____

> *Permit it to be so now, for it becomes us to fulfill*
> *all righteousness.* (Matthew 3:15)

Jesus permitted what he did not need in order to show us what we *do* need: a new relationship with God through repentance and baptism. Keep in mind that some things are permitted in order for a larger purpose to be fulfilled. Our lives are a peculiar mixture of occurrences from which we can discern lessons we need to learn.

In what ways have you made sacrifices to benefit others in fulfilling their life's desire?

_____

_____

_____

_____

_____

_____

_____

_____

_____

_____

> *It is written, 'Man shall not live by bread alone, but by every word that proceeds from the mouth of God.'* (Matthew 4:4)

Our appetite, when not satisfied, becomes a source of temptation that won't be denied. Jesus' words are rooted in an incident that makes us aware that appetite is only an instrument. We do not live by our appetite alone but by that which is larger, mightier, and closer to home. Find in God's word comfort and follow the light that brightens your way today.

What discipline is required for you to put on hold the appetite that if fulfilled would cause you to lose control?

It is written again, 'You shall not tempt the LORD your God.'
(Matthew 4:7)

Ambition is about achievement at its best and superiority at its worst. Be careful in your quest to rise to the heights of your ambition, for in doing so you might test God. Testing God entails thinking that your own plans and desires are more important than God's. God's desires have been disclosed. Trust and embrace what is written.

How are you tempted to put God to the test when your ambition will not let you rest?

_____

_____

_____

_____

_____

_____

_____

_____

_____

Get behind me, Satan! For it is written, 'You shall worship the Lord your God . . .' (Matthew 4:10)

Allegiance is about commitment, fidelity, and loyalty. Commit your way to the Lord and be faithful each day. Worship God only and follow God's way. Keep life in perspective by following God's instructions. When we worship the Lord, we inevitably put Satan behind us. There is no space left for Satan in our lives.

What do you need to refuse if you are to give the Lord first place rather than let something else occupy that precious space?

_____

_____

_____

_____

_____

_____

_____

_____

_____

_____

_____

> '. . . *And serve him only.*' (Matthew 4:10)

Fidelity is difficult. Each day we face challenges to fidelity. Sometimes it seems that just when you have your life under control, the attacks come. You find yourself faced with a choice to continue on the good path or to defect. When your allegiance is tested, it can be tough to remember whom you serve, but these are the times when we must *most* remember whom we serve.

What would it take for you to resolve right now to serve God only and always?

_____

_____

_____

_____

_____

_____

_____

_____

_____

_____

_____

Repent, for the kingdom of heaven is at hand. (Matthew 4:17)

"Repent" is an extraordinary word. It means both going back and going beyond. On the one hand, repentance calls us to return to God. We have left God by not following what we were told would fulfill us. On the other hand, repentance calls us to go beyond ourselves. We get so comfortable with the life we mold that we find it difficult to break the hold that we have permitted to control us. Let's get back to God and get beyond ourselves so that we can live a life that is completely fulfilled, reordering our priorities and reorganizing our lives, putting God first, exposing our lies.

What do you need to do to get beyond yourself and get back to God?

Follow me, and I will make you fishers of men. (Matthew 4:19)

To be made into what you can be is what the Lord promises as he says, "Come after me." Here is an invitation for you to consider what you will do with your life. Come and be made into all you can be. It is your choice to accept or decline. This invitation is extended to those who are ready to give their all.

What would it take for you to accept the invitation of a lifetime to be a part of a divine purpose?

_____

_____

_____

_____

_____

_____

_____

_____

_____

_____

_____

THE SERMON ON THE MOUNT IS A COMPILATION OF the teachings of Jesus that serve to to inform and teach those who would be disciples and followers of Christ. This Sermon begins with what are called the Beatitudes. Jesus cites nine situations of life that everyone faces. Throughout his teachings, Jesus provides a directive to help determine the right perspective. Here are attitudes that will help you face life with all its distress. In trusting Jesus' words and wisdom, you will be blessed.

The selections for January 10–April 5 focus on Jesus' words and teachings offered in The Sermon on the Mount.

Blessed are the poor in spirit, for theirs is the kingdom of heaven.
(Matthew 5:3)

Those who are aware of their limitations and inadequacies have accessible to them an unlimited resource to make up for any deficit. Unlimited resources are available to you when you acknowledge what you can't do. What you need in order to manage life is available to you in Christ.

What is the limitation you need to acknowledge in order to put yourself in position to receive the benefits of the Lord's invitation?

_____

_____

_____

_____

_____

_____

_____

_____

_____

_____

Blessed are those who mourn, for they shall be comforted.
(Matthew 5:4)

Mourning is an inevitable part of living, for there is no way to live without losing what we would rather not let go: family, friends, life, time, youth, to name a few. We all experience a loss of some kind during our lives. Consider the losses you have endured and how they all have emptied your life. What you need to manage life when you mourn is the confidence that you will find comfort. God gives us assurance to let us know that what we need is near.

What comfort is available to you to help you with the losses you experience along life's way?

_____

_____

_____

_____

_____

_____

_____

_____

_____

_____

> *Blessed are the meek, for they shall inherit the earth.*
> (Matthew 5:5)

Do not confuse meekness with weakness, for they are definitely not the same. Being meek means that you manage your attitude, behavior, and pattern of thought regardless of the situations in life in which you find yourself. When you take charge of managing yourself, you will automatically receive as a gift what others seek. Strange as it may seem, what we most pursue is a byproduct that accrues to us because of something else we do.

How can you better manage your attitude, behavior, and thought patterns to receive the result you most desire?

_____

_____

_____

_____

_____

_____

_____

_____

Blessed are they who hunger and thirst after righteousness, for they shall be filled. (Matthew 5:6)

There is no desire without the possibility of fulfillment. Imagine how frustrating life would be if what you desired just couldn't be. It is good to know that where there is desire, there is the possibility of fulfillment. Those who crave righteousness can have their desire and hunger satisfied.

In what way do you hunger and thirst after righteousness? In what way do you find your desire being fulfilled?

_____

_____

_____

_____

_____

_____

_____

_____

_____

_____

Blessed are the merciful, for they shall obtain mercy.
(Matthew 5:7)

It is one of the facts of life that we get what we give. Give what you want to receive and trust God to provide what you need. Mercy is withholding what people deserve in order to give them another chance. We all need second chances, and thus we should be prepared to grant them.

In what ways have you been merciful and received mercy in return?

_____

_____

_____

_____

_____

_____

_____

_____

_____

_____

_____

> *Blessed are the pure in heart, for they shall see God.*
> (Matthew 5:8)

There is a clear relationship between purity of affection and singleness of direction. And there is in turn a relationship between focused direction and clarity of perception. Perception is determined by affection. Our eyes see what our hearts call to mind. So when the heart is impure, it is difficult to see the sublime. Today we commemorate the life of one whose singleness of direction was determined by his affection, his love for God and neighbor. God is clearly seen when the heart is pure, when it is free from the contamination that obscures.

What do you need to do to free your heart from the impurity that would keep you from seeing God?

Blessed are the peacemakers, for they shall be called the children of God. (Matthew 5:9)

Peace requires intentional effort. You have to work hard to bring into being the tranquility that you dream of seeing. What you will receive as a result of your efforts will be worth enduring all of the hardships you may have to face.

When you consider the conflict that is part of your life, in what ways can you be a peacemaker?

JANUARY 17 🌿

Blessed are they who are persecuted for righteousness' sake, for theirs is the kingdom of heaven. (Matthew 5:10)

Those who are persecuted for that which is just inherit a priceless treasure. You have available unlimited resources to deal with any abuse. So when you are mistreated for doing what is right, remember the kingdom of heaven is on your side.

In what ways has faith strengthened your resolve to endure what you were suffering when you were unjustly treated?

_____

_____

_____

_____

_____

_____

_____

_____

Blessed are you, when men shall revile you, and persecute you, and say all manner of evil against you falsely, for my sake. Rejoice, and be exceeding glad: for great is your reward in heaven, for they so persecuted the prophets before you.
(Matthew 5:11-12)

Imagine willful suffering yielding exceeding joy. It does not seem to make sense. When attempting to see beyond the brutality to which we may fall victim, it helps to recall the examples of others whose lives remind us that our suffering will not end in futility.

How do faith and the example of others help you to persevere when you are mistreated?

You are the salt of the earth: but if the salt has lost its savor,
wherewith shall it be salted? It is thenceforth good for nothing,
but to be cast out, and to be trodden under the foot of men.
(Matthew 5:13)

Identity and function are tied together. You do what you are, and you are what you do. Jesus tells us who we are so that we can fulfill our purpose for being. As salt flavors, cleanses, and cures, we have the capacity to do the same. Be who you are in Christ, one who enhances the taste of life, cleanses the filth from life, and cures the ills of life.

In what ways can you flavor, cleanse, and cure the situations you face?

> *You are the light of the world. A city that is set on a hill cannot be hid.* (Matthew 5:14)

Light does at least three things. First, light exposes what is present but is in danger of being overlooked. Second, light energizes the growth potential of what's alive. Third, light attracts in a single direction what it energizes toward growth. Be who you are as light, dispelling the gloom of life, sparking the growth of life, and positively directing the flow of life.

In what ways can you dispel the darkness, spark the growth, and direct the flow of life for yourself and others?

_____

_____

_____

_____

_____

_____

_____

_____

_____

Neither do men light a candle, and put it under a bushel, but on a candlestick; and it gives light to all that are in the house.
(Matthew 5:15)

Light dispels darkness, penetrates haziness, and illumines vagueness so that all can see clearly what has been hidden. Light's function is to reveal what we know we must. So from this time forward, let your light shine. Accept the responsibilities that come with your faith.

What do you need to do to emit what is the best in you so that you can be what others need to see?

_____

_____

_____

_____

_____

_____

_____

_____

_____

Let your light so shine before men, that they may see your good works, and glorify your Father which is in heaven.
(Matthew 5:16)

You are admonished to be what you reflect so that you can model for others the life Jesus would have you live. In order for this to happen, your light must shine brightly so that all who see your image will come to know the God you worship. Your witness can make a difference for those who are still searching in the darkness.

How can you let your light shine so that people will know that your life is wrapped up with what is sublime?

_____

_____

_____

_____

_____

_____

_____

_____

Think not that I am come to destroy the law, or the prophets: I am not come to destroy but to fulfill. (Matthew 5:17)

Jesus does not destroy what preceded him in order to point to what comes after him. Rather, he recognizes what has gone before as the precursor of what follows. The law and the teachings are not to be disconnected from the example Jesus set. They are part of the same fabric. Like Jesus, we have the opportunity each day to build on what has gone before.

How do you make the most of what has happened before in order to fulfill your life now?

_____

_____

_____

_____

_____

_____

_____

_____

For verily I say unto you, till heaven and earth pass, one jot or one tittle shall in no wise pass from the law, till all be fulfilled.
(Matthew 5:18)

What a guarantee! Of all the things of which you can be sure, the Word of God is the only thing that is absolutely pure. You can count on what is disclosed in its sacred pages to equip you to handle anything that happens. It has been tried and proven true. It continues to provide insight for all who seek to understand its priceless principles and timeless truths.

In what way are you comforted by the certainty that you can rely on the Word of the Lord?

_____

_____

_____

_____

_____

_____

_____

_____

_____

> *Whosoever therefore shall break one of these least*
> *commandments, and shall teach men so, shall be called*
> *the least in the kingdom of heaven: but whosoever shall do*
> *and teach them, the same shall be called great in the*
> *kingdom of heaven.* (Matthew 5:19)

In whose eyes do you want to be held in highest regard? We seek to please those whose admiration we desire. Strange, don't you think, that we are willing to do some less-than-desirable things to please persons whose acceptance we seek? Choose wisely whom you are willing to gratify, for in the long run it may not satisfy the goals of your life.

What choices do you need to make to comply with the direction you want your life to take?

_____

_____

_____

_____

_____

_____

_____

_____

For I say to you, that except your righteousness exceed the righteousness of the scribes and Pharisees, you shall in no case enter into the kingdom of heaven. (Matthew 5:20)

At least two things are required for our soul's health: an awareness of our inadequacy and a realization of our justification in, by, and through a sacrifice made for us. There is no health without confession and surrender. Confession acknowledges what we have done, and surrender accepts what the sacrifice for us has won. Jesus did for us what we could not do for ourselves, thereby becoming for us what we could not become without him.

What confession will you make today as you receive the benefits of the sacrifice the Lord makes?

_____

_____

_____

_____

_____

_____

_____

_____

You have heard that it was said by them of old time, you shall not kill; and whosoever shall kill shall be in danger of the judgment: But I say unto you, that whosoever is angry with his brother without a cause shall be in danger of the judgment: and whosoever shall say to his brother, Raca, shall be in danger of the council: but whosoever shall say, thou fool, shall be in danger of hell fire. (Matthew 5:21-22)

When you permit anger to determine your actions, you run the risk of doing what is ungodly and disgraceful. Manage the swelling tide of emotions that engulf you, when provoked, so that you can respond in a way that will prevent the escalation of tensions. How often in the heat of passion have we permitted something to fuel negative behavior?

What fuels your passion? What do you need to control?

_____

_____

_____

_____

_____

_____

_____

_____

Therefore, if you bring a gift to the altar, and there remember that your brother has ought against you; leave there your gift before the altar, and go your way; first be reconciled to your brother, and then come and offer your gift. (Matthew 5:23-24)

Our relationship with God finds expression first in our connections with one another. We cannot ignore our human obligations to one another under the guise of worshiping God. The two are inextricably intertwined. You cannot love God and hate what God has created, for what God has made is also a reflection of who God is.

Examine your connections with others. Are there relationships that need reconciliation? How will you pursue that reconciliation?

_____

_____

_____

_____

_____

_____

_____

_____

_____

_____

Agree with your adversary quickly, while you are in the way with him; lest at any time the adversary deliver you to the judge, and the judge deliver you to the officer, and you be cast into prison.
(Matthew 5:25)

Here is practical, sound advice that has been expressed in the cliché "discretion is the better part of valor." This is good common sense. After all, some disagreements just don't make sense. Consider those situations in which quickly agreeing is your best defense.

In what situations do you need to agree quickly in order to avoid furthering conflict?

_____

_____

_____

_____

_____

_____

_____

_____

_____

_____

_____

You have heard that it was said of them of old time, you shall not commit adultery: But I say unto you, that whosoever looks on a woman to lust after her has already committed adultery in his heart. (Matthew 5:27-28)

The standards of the Lord raise the bar, causing us to consider the connection between our thoughts and behavior. As we think, so we are. The thought precedes the act, and the act is nothing more than an extension of the thought. The old proverb says, "As a person thinks, so is he or she."

When and how have your thoughts directed or influenced your behavior negatively?

_____

_____

_____

_____

_____

_____

_____

_____

_____

And if your right eye offend you, pluck it out, and cast it from you: for it is profitable for you that one of your members should perish, and not that your whole body should be cast into hell.
(Matthew 5:29)

There are times when we miss what we want most because a part of our life is out of control. One damaging feature can cancel a positive result. Bring your passions into conformity with the purposes of God. In order to gain what you want and miss what you don't want, you may have to give up something. Exclude what would keep you from achieving your heavenly best so as not to miss what is more important than anything else.

What do you need to exclude in order to gain what you want and miss what you don't want?

_____

_____

_____

_____

_____

_____

_____

_____

But let your communication be yes, or no; for whatsoever is more than these comes from evil. (Matthew 5:37)

False and irreverent oaths profane what is godly. All that is required is that your "yes" mean yes and your "no" mean no. Anything more is ill advised. Often we are tempted by people to do or say what we ought to avoid doing or saying. That is where it all begins: with being counterfeit and impudent when we try to win what we want from others to validate us in the end. If people are not going to believe you, they will not believe you regardless of what you do or say. All that is required is that you do what you know to do as you go your way.

How have you been tempted to make oaths that profane what is godly? How can you fight this temptation?

_____

_____

_____

_____

_____

_____

_____

_____

_____

But I say unto you, love your enemies, bless them that curse you, do good to them that hate you, and pray for them which despitefully use you, and persecute you: that you may be the children of your Father which is in heaven: for he makes his sun to rise on the evil and on the good, and sends rain on the just and on the unjust. (Matthew 5:44-45)

Determine your attitude and behavior toward those who have hurt, harmed, or offended you. Make a choice about how you handle yourself, which is about all you can do. You can permit what happens to control you, or you can decide that *you* will decide what you are going do. In so doing, you define yourself, regardless of difficult dilemmas, and confirm your character, regardless of circumstances.

How will you determine to deal with those who harm, hurt, or offend you?

_____

_____

_____

_____

_____

_____

_____

Be perfect, as your Father in heaven is perfect. (Matthew 5:48)

"Perfect" carries with it connotations that leave us with a sense of our deficiencies, for the standard by which we are measured leaves us feeling inadequate. But Jesus' call to be "perfect" is a positive and motivating call, not one to make us feel burdened. Striving after perfection is striving after God because God is perfect. God is characterized as perfect because God is complete. There is nothing lacking in God. When we strive in this sense to be "perfect," to be complete, we are striving after God. As creatures made in God's image and fashioned in God's likeness, we strive to fulfill our capacity to be complete, to be whole.

In what ways do you need to strive to be complete and whole so as to become more like God?

_____

_____

_____

_____

_____

_____

_____

_____

*Take heed that you do not your alms before men, to be seen
of them: otherwise you have no reward of your Father
which is in heaven.* (Matthew 6:1)

Do what you do from the heart because of your love for God, not
from a need to be seen by others. When you do what you do for
people, you forfeit your reward from God. When you do what you
do for God, you forfeit your reward from people. The reason you
do what you do will determine the reward you receive. You must
decide whose reward is most important.

How will you determine to give what you give because of God
rather than people?

_____

_____

_____

_____

_____

_____

_____

_____

Therefore, when you give, do not sound a trumpet as the hypocrites do in the synagogues and in the streets, that they may have glory of men. Verily I say to you, they have their reward.
(Matthew 6:2)

Publicizing faithfulness to call attention to one's self is considered an offense to God. Do what you do because you have chosen to do it, not because you are starved for recognition and will do whatever you can to get it. Give as an expression of appreciation, not as an attempt to get attention. What would you give if no one knew what you gave? Would you give of your best or just a little thing?

Would you give what you give if no one knew about it? Is there room for growth?

_____

_____

_____

_____

_____

_____

_____

_____

But when you give, let not your left hand know what your right hand is doing, that your giving may be in secret: and thy Father who sees in secret shall reward you openly. (Matthew 6:3-4)

Giving is to be done freely and spontaneously out of the graciousness of the heart, commensurate with the blessings you have received. Perhaps you have experienced what others have experienced, namely that the more you give, the more that comes back to you. Give with a grateful heart. Give to the holy God.

What would it take for you to decide to give without seeking public recognition for your gift?

_____

_____

_____

_____

_____

_____

_____

_____

*And when you pray, do not be as the hypocrites: for they love
to pray standing in the synagogues and in the corners of
the streets, that they may be seen of men. Verily I say
unto you, they have their reward. (Matthew 6:5)*

Prayer is neither for show nor for the answers received. It is for
communion with the One in whom we believe. The will of God is
discovered in prayer, and it is in prayer where we find our connection with God. The need to be seen should not get in the way of
this important connection. Remember to keep your focus not on
others but on God so that when you pray you can connect with
God in a special way.

What stimulates your desire for prayer?

_____

_____

_____

_____

_____

_____

_____

_____

_____

*But when you pray, enter into thy closet, and when you have
shut the door, pray to the Father which is in secret; and the
Father which sees in secret shall reward you openly.*
(Matthew 6:6)

As noted yesterday, the purpose of prayer is for those who believe
in communion to commune with God. We can find in God all we
need. In the secret place of the cherished heart, we discover the
mind and the heart of God. Set aside a place where you can go to
get away and come to know that God is present in all of life's
changing scenes. God is present to give us courage for our circumstance, direction for our difficulty, and strength for our situation.

Have you set aside a place where you can connect with God
through prayer during your day? What has been your experience?

_____

_____

_____

_____

_____

_____

_____

_____

When you pray, use not vain repetitions, as the heathen do: for
they think that they shall be heard for their much speaking.
(Matthew 6:7)

Speak sincerely to God. It doesn't take much. Simply state what
burdens your heart; then wait and listen for the voice of God. You
can hear it in the silence as you commune with God. God speaks
by the power of the Holy Spirit through circumstances, through
people of faith, and through the Bible. God can also speak to us in
silent moments, but we must take the initiative to seek God sincerely, not through vain repetition.

Speak to God sincerely today. What is God saying in some situation that you are facing?

_____

_____

_____

_____

_____

_____

_____

_____

Be not like them: for your Father knows what things you need before you ask. (Matthew 6:8)

Prayer is more of an expression about our awareness of God and our connection to God rather than the information we impart about ourselves to God. Since God is omniscient, all we need to do is posture ourselves to perceive the powerful, pervasive presence of the Lord in our midst. God knows what we need. It is our awareness of the presence of the Lord that will make the difference in the way we handle what we face.

In what ways can you begin to present yourself to the Lord in prayer without a lot of excessive talking about what the Lord already knows?

_____

_____

_____

_____

_____

_____

_____

_____

After this manner pray: Our Father which is in heaven.
(Matthew 6:9)

Jesus teaches us with this model prayer about the nature of the One whose love and care we can depend on every moment of every day. Prayer addresses as it acknowledges. Begin praying by addressing the Lord as you acknowledge who you believe God to be. Call on the Lord in the way you have come to know the Lord's presence in your life.

How would you address the Lord given the way you have come to know the Lord in your life? How is God like a parent to you?

_____

_____

_____

_____

_____

_____

_____

_____

_____

_____

Hallowed be your name. (Matthew 6:9)

The name of the Lord, which depicts the nature and character of God, is sacred. The Lord's name is not to be taken in vain but is to be used only in the most holy of ways. Reverence for God's name is synonymous with respect for God. God's name reflects God's character and the essence of God's nature. Affirm respect for God by reverencing God's name. When you call on the Lord in the way you have come to know God, announce your admiration with awe.

How can you make obvious your respect for the designation you use to refer to God, whether you call the Lord, Shepherd, Friend, or Father?

_____

_____

_____

_____

_____

_____

_____

_____

_____

_____

_____

_____

FEBRUARY 13 ❦

> *Your kingdom come.* (Matthew 6:10)

Establish your authority, God, where we live. This is the hope of believers who trust in their Lord's purpose. It is reassuring to embrace the truth that in the midst of obvious and rampant uncertainty God has an intention that will work in our best interest through all of life's changing scenes, whether good or bad, happy or sad, sick or healthy, impoverished or abundant.

What will it take for you to believe and embrace that God is working for your good in everything that happens so that you can pray, "Your kingdom come"?

FEBRUARY 14 ❦

Your will be done in earth, as it is in heaven. (Matthew 6:10)

The conformity of our lives to the will of God promotes the accomplishment of God's plan for creation. There is a design for life beyond what we see that begs us to get in touch with what can be. Too often we are limited in our perception. We short-circuit the possibilities, forgetting that the will of God is far more ambitious than what we can imagine.

What would it take for you to be able to say, "Lord, I embrace your will today"? What possibilities have you not been noticing?

_____

_____

_____

_____

_____

_____

_____

_____

_____

_____

Give us this day our daily bread. (Matthew 6:11)

Expression of our daily need is essential, if for no other reason than to let us know that God cares about us. We ask with confidence that God will indeed provide. We ask in faith, acknowledging the One who provides daily bread, the One who meets our needs.

In what ways does God provide for your needs each day?

_____

_____

_____

_____

_____

_____

_____

_____

_____

_____

And forgive us our debts, as we forgive our debtors.
(Matthew 6:12)

In admitting what we have done, we raise our awareness to understand others who have caused us harm. As we confess, we drop our defenses against those who have robbed us of something. We all need pardon, and so do others. What we receive, we give. In one breath as you pray, acknowledge your need to be forgiven as you affirm your need to forgive others.

For what do you need forgiveness, and for what do you need to forgive others?

_____

_____

_____

_____

_____

_____

_____

_____

_____

And lead us not into temptation, but deliver us from evil.
(Matthew 6:13)

Lord, keep us from the enticements that would cause us to fall. Free us from the wickedness that beckons during the course of earthly life. We all need to be aware of what we face so that we will not be surprised or unprepared, so that we can avoid evil when it crosses our path, as surely it will.

From what kind of temptation do you need to be kept? What evil do you most desire to avoid?

_____

_____

_____

_____

_____

_____

_____

_____

_____

_____

_____

*For thine is the kingdom, and the power, and the glory, forever.
Amen.* (Matthew 6:13)

Have confidence in the ultimate plan and purpose of God by acknowledging God's authority, capability, and grandeur. When you consider that God is active in the affairs of the world, you can trust in the power God possesses to bring to pass what God desires. Conclude your prayer on a note of assurance with an affirmation of faith that God is present. God is bringing to pass something that will last forever.

What does it mean to you and to your faith to know that God's kingdom, power, and glory are forever?

_____

_____

_____

_____

_____

_____

_____

_____

_____

For if you forgive people their trespasses, your heavenly Father will also forgive you. (Matthew 6:14)

There is a direct correlation between how we respond to people and how the Lord responds to us. By freeing yourself of the burden of being hurt, by forgiving others, you are also freed from the burden of having hurt God. The two are like opposite sides of the same coin. They go together as an inseparable piece of cloth, one side forming the warp and the other the woof.

How hard is it for you to forgive others?

_____

_____

_____

_____

_____

_____

_____

_____

_____

_____

_____

But if you do not forgive people their trespasses, neither will your Father forgive your trespasses. (Matthew 6:15)

When you choose to carry the burden of your hurts, the Lord permits you to carry the burden of having hurt the Lord. You give what you receive. There is no way to accept the forgiveness of God without forgiving others. When we do not forgive, we have not accepted the forgiveness that we have been given. We become what we have received, forgiving as we have been forgiven.

Why is it difficult for you to forgive others as you embrace the forgiveness of God?

Moreover when you fast, be not as the hypocrites, of a sad countenance: for they disfigure their faces, that they may appear unto men to fast. Verily I say unto you, they have their reward.
(Matthew 6:16)

Jesus condemns doing what you do to call attention to yourself. Do what you do to honor God rather than to be seen of people. Jesus suggests that the misuse of discipline to attract attention to one's self is merely acting and pretending. The purpose of spiritual discipline is to get better connected to the Lord, not to flaunt what one is doing.

In what ways have you called attention to yourself? How have you used spiritual disciplines as a means of calling attention to yourself?

When you fast, anoint your head, and wash your face; that
you appear not unto people to fast, but unto your Father
which is in secret: and your Father, which sees in secret,
shall reward you openly. (Matthew 6:17-18)

Spiritual disciplines express a person's desire to get closer to God.
The outward act merely reflects the inward attitude. Exercise
restraint as a way of stimulating your allegiance, strengthening
your commitment. Do what you do to honor God without display,
and the Lord will reward you openly and abundantly.

What spiritual discipline can you practice regularly to strengthen
your relationship with the Lord?

_____

_____

_____

_____

_____

_____

_____

_____

_____

_____

Lay not up for yourselves treasure upon earth, where moth and rust do corrupt, and where thieves break through and steal.
(Matthew 6:19)

These words from Jesus provide sound advice about our attachment to the stuff we accumulate in life. We are prone to become overly attached to things we ultimately can't keep. Jesus reminds us that all the treasures stored on earth are temporary. They are at the mercy of moth, rust, and thieves. They will either leave us, or we will leave them. Put your treasures in proper perspective. The reality is that we cannot keep what we treasure on earth forever.

What are your earthly treasures? How can you develop a healthy perspective on them?

_____

_____

_____

_____

_____

_____

_____

_____

> *But lay up for yourselves treasures in heaven, where neither*
> *moth nor rust does corrupt, and where thieves do not*
> *break through nor steal.* (Matthew 6:20)

The crucial concern in regard to treasures is what type they are and where they are stored. You have treasures that are far more valuable than things, and these treasures should be stored in a safe place. Invest in what you cannot lose. Invest in those intangible realities that make of life meaningful and significant. Invest in faith, and you will find security in the future.

How can you begin today to build the treasure of faith that stores what is important for you in a safe place?

_____

_____

_____

_____

_____

_____

_____

_____

_____

> *For where your treasure is, there will your heart be also.*
> (Matthew 6:21)

Treasure and heart are curiously connected. When you consider the treasure that is important to you, notice that your heart is wrapped up in it too. You invest in what you love, and you love that in which you invest. You put your money where your heart is, and your heart is where you put your wealth.

What do you treasure? What does your treasure say about your heart? What does your heart say about your treasure?

_____

_____

_____

_____

_____

_____

_____

_____

_____

_____

The light of the body is the eye: if therefore your eye be single,
your whole body shall be full of light. (Matthew 6:22)

Devotion to God fills one's life with light. The eye is the window for the light. Singularity of focus provides what is indispensable—illumination and direction. Who is it who does not need more light? You can have more light today. Embrace the Lord in all you do. God will provide all the light you need.

What do you need to do to let more of the light of the Lord fill your life?

_____

_____

_____

_____

_____

_____

_____

_____

_____

_____

> *But if your eye be evil, your whole body shall be*
> *full of darkness.* (Matthew 6:23)

Just as life is shrouded in darkness when one is blind, so God is hidden by shadows when one is distracted by iniquity. Evil can get in the way of our following God. We expose ourselves to iniquity when we lean to our own way and allow ourselves to be controlled by impulses that lead us astray, even though we know what is right. Darkness can come even in the light of day.

Is there sin in your life that obscures the light of God?

_____

_____

_____

_____

_____

_____

_____

_____

_____

_____

If therefore the light that is in you be darkness, how great is that darkness! (Matthew 6:23)

If what should be bright in you is dim, then your light is weak and fails to glow. You then become the opposite of what you are supposed to be, emitting darkness instead of light, losing opportunities to help others to see. How tragic it is when we fail to become what we are intended to be.

How has your life been altered because you chose darkness? How will you determine to replace the darkness with light?

_____

_____

_____

_____

_____

_____

_____

_____

_____

_____

_____

> No one can serve two masters: for either he will hate
> the one, and love the other; or else he will hold to the one,
> and despise the other. (Matthew 6:24a)

It has been said that Christ is Lord of all or Christ is not Lord at all. It is difficult, it seems, to admit that we accept the Lord in pieces and bits. We like a little of this and none of that or some of that and none of this. But if Christ is Lord of all, it is for us to give him all of our selves, all of our loyalty.

In what way do you accept what you like as you ignore what you don't like about what the Lord instructs?

_____

_____

_____

_____

_____

_____

_____

_____

_____

> *You cannot serve God and mammon.* (Matthew 6:24b)

Money is important, to be sure. It can be used for many good and noble purposes. But when it becomes the focus of our desires and our energies, it is a distraction, plain and simple. Jesus tells us that money competes with God for our loyalty and service. We need to decide each day whether God or mammon will win out.

What is it that truly makes you happy, that provides you with a deep sense of inner joy, of peace that passes understanding? Can these things be purchased?

_____

_____

_____

_____

_____

_____

_____

_____

_____

> *Therefore I say unto you, take no thought for your life, what*
> *you shall eat, or what you shall drink; nor yet for your*
> *body, what you shall put on.* (Matthew 6:25)

The antidote for anxiety is assurance. Live, relying on the providential care woven into the fabric of existence, trusting the way you have come so far. We worry needlessly about what we cannot control. We expend needless time and energy trying to get a hold of things that are better left to God, who will provide.

In what areas of life are you most anxious, most worried about things you cannot control?

_____

_____

_____

_____

_____

_____

_____

_____

_____

_____

_____

Is not life more than meat, and the body more than raiment?
(Matthew 6:25)

Life is more than food and clothing. Life is so much more than what we are merely able to see. We are far more than what we eat or wear; our worth is not determined by what we accumulate here. Redirect the focus of your concern to deal with the important priorities of life.

How can you realize that there is more to life than what you eat or wear?

_____

_____

_____

_____

_____

_____

_____

_____

_____

Behold the fowls of the air: for they sow not, neither do they reap, nor gather into barns; yet your heavenly Father feeds them.
(Matthew 6:26)

Consider those who are in God's hands. They fare quite well, even though it seems that so much—the wind and the rain and more—is beyond their control. They are small, insignificant in the eyes of the world. But God feeds them, cares for them during their time of life. Nothing escapes God's watchful eye. Caring takes place in everyday places and in common ways. Just take a look all around and you will see ample evidence of God's caring for the creation and all that is therein.

How does the natural world around you testify to God's watchful eye over creation?

_____

_____

_____

_____

_____

_____

_____

_____

Are you not much better than they? (Matthew 6:26)

Lessons from what we see around us are constant reminders that our value to God is greater than we know. God treasures us. We can cope with what we face knowing that built into the fabric of existence is the assurance that God continually provides for us. We can trust even in our uncertainty that we have what we need to provide assurance that God loves and cares for us.

How can you value your worth as God values you rather than the way others do?

_____

_____

_____

_____

_____

_____

_____

_____

_____

_____

Which of you by taking thought can add one cubit to his stature?
(Matthew 6:27)

Anxiety is an exercise in futility. All it does is accent your fragility. So why do you continue to let worry dictate your behavior and consume your energy? You have available everything you need in Jesus' words of life. You cannot change anything by worrying, so why waste your time? Why not use your energy in wholesome, productive ways instead of wasting it on worry?

What do you need to do to get beyond needless worrying about what you cannot change?

_____

_____

_____

_____

_____

_____

_____

_____

_____

And why take you thought for raiment? Consider the lilies of the field, how they toil not, neither do they spin. (Matthew 6:28)

What a waste to spend your energy foolishly considering inconsequential matters. Nature evidences the kind of trust we can have in the care of God for creation. Look around and see just what is built into the fabric of life for humanity. We have all we need to settle our doubts and calm our fears. Find the beauty around you. And take from it confidence that God cares for you more than you can imagine.

What observations can you make in life that afford you the opportunity to know that God's provisions abound?

_____

_____

_____

_____

_____

_____

_____

_____

_____

And yet I say to you, that even Solomon in all his glory was not arrayed like one of these. (Matthew 6:29)

One of the richest and wisest persons in the world was not adorned any better than God's natural creation. What a wonderful thought to ponder when we are perplexed about what causes us to be anxious. The wealthiest person cannot take care of himself or herself any better than God can take care of creation. We can count on the Lord's provision to make available what we need.

What would it take for you to believe that God cares for you?

_____

_____

_____

_____

_____

_____

_____

_____

_____

_____

*Wherefore, if God so clothe the grass of the field, which today is,
and tomorrow is cast into the oven, shall he not much more
clothe you, O you of little faith?* (Matthew 6:30)

Anxiety is connected to lack of faith. The only antidote for anxiety is
assurance. Jesus gives the assurance that God cares, citing an instance
in nature where God's care can be seen. We need to learn to trust
God's providential care for our needs, as does the grass of the field.

What keeps you from trusting in the providential care of God in
your life?

_____

_____

_____

_____

_____

_____

_____

_____

_____

Therefore take no thought, saying, What shall we eat? or, What shall we drink? or, With what shall we be clothed?
(Matthew 6:31)

We are admonished to face uncertainty without frustration. These are challenging words. When things look bleak, our human nature is to doubt instead of to trust. Jesus' words here should not be taken to mean we should never make plans to provide for ourselves. But often these plans are insufficient. We are fragile beings. When confronted by challenges, however, we display our faith by remaining calm, confident in God's plan and provisions, difficult though that may be.

How can you direct your thougths to diminish your frustration about uncertainty?

_____

_____

_____

_____

_____

_____

_____

_____

_____

> *. . . for your heavenly Father knows that you have need
> of these things.* (Matthew 6:32)

You can be confident that God's provisions for your needs are sure.
Just as creation depends on God's care, so we can count on God to
be there for us. God knows what we need. This should free us to
pursue the things of God instead of the things of the world. The
challenge we face is to release our minds and spirits of trivial matters so that we can pursue God's priorities.

How can you begin to put your trust completely in God amid a
culture of anxiety that says you need to hoard?

_____

_____

_____

_____

_____

_____

_____

_____

_____

But seek you first the kingdom of God, and his righteousness;
and all these things shall be added unto you. (Matthew 6:33)

The Lord promises that if you get your priorities straight, all that you seek will be added to you. What we spend our time chasing is a by-product of something else. We look for security in all that we do, only to discover that peace of mind eludes us. We keep on striving only to discover that the more we get, the more anxiety we uncover. For the things we get never really satisfy; they simply fill a gap and for only a brief moment. To have the real security you want, seek God first.

In what way can you begin to make God the first priority in your life?

_____

_____

_____

_____

_____

_____

_____

_____

Take therefore no thought for tomorrow: for tomorrow shall take thought for the things of itself. (Matthew 6:34)

One day at a time is all we can live. Each moment is an eternity in itself. Cherish each moment and savor each day, realizing each blessing that comes your way. Tomorrow will take care of itself. This is a startling notion. Jesus knew that if we concern ourselves with tomorrow, we will miss the opportunities of today. Tomorrow will be here soon enough. So take advantage of today while it lasts.

In what way can you begin to embrace each day in order not merely to get through it but to make the most of it?

_____

_____

_____

_____

_____

_____

_____

_____

_____

_____

Sufficient unto the day is the evil thereof. (Matthew 6:34)

In each twenty-four-hour period, handle what you can. Leave the rest for another day. Each day has enough trouble of its own, so it does not make sense to carry trouble from one day to the next. Jesus' practical wisdom shines through here. Face each day. Take life as it comes. You will find the resources you need and more.

What can you do to begin handling only the trouble that comes with a single day rather than piling on trouble day after day?

_____

_____

_____

_____

_____

_____

_____

_____

_____

Judge not, that you be not judged. (Matthew 7:1)

Determining the inner motives of another is difficult at best, thus we are admonished to avoid succumbing to this temptation. However sure we may be, we could be wrong about the other person. When you think about it, who is really in a position to know all that has transpired in a person's life to cause them to be as they are? Perhaps another person is angry or sad for reasons we don't understand. So don't judge too quickly. Better yet, don't judge at all.

Are there persons in your life right now about whom you have made judgments that may not be fair? How will you seek to make things right?

_____

_____

_____

_____

_____

_____

_____

_____

_____

_____

For with what judgment you judge, you shall be judged: and with what measure you mete, it shall be measured to you again.
(Matthew 7:2)

You will be dealt with in the same spirit, by the same measure, according to the same truth and generosity you have shown. Whatever criterion we use to determine the sincerity of others will be used to determine our sincerity. Could you stand to be judged by the standard by which you judge others?

What adjustments in the way you form an opinion do you need to make in order to give people the benefit of doubt?

*And why behold the mote that is in your brother's eye, and do
not consider the beam that is in your own?* (Matthew 7:3)

It is our human nature it seems to see the little things that are
wrong with others as we ignore the big things in ourselves. So
before you judge someone else, take another look at yourself.
Maybe we cannot be heard by those with whom we want to share
because of the critical stance we take toward them. Let us not neglect to turn the mirror on ourselves. It's easier to improve our own
behavior than it is to control the behavior of others.

How can you resolve to focus on yourself and what needs to
change about you, rather than focusing on others and what you
think ought to change about them?

_____

_____

_____

_____

_____

_____

_____

_____

_____

Or how will you say to your brother, let me pull out the mote in your eye; and, behold, a beam is in your own eye? (Matthew 7:4)

And as long as our own lives leave plenty of room for improvement, we have little chance of influencing others. Thus, how presumptuous it is of us to correct someone else without correcting ourselves! Correcting the faults of others can be a way of trying to ignore or hide our own faults. So before taking action against another, make sure your eyes are clear of any obstacles that may be preventing you from having a clear view.

In what way have you tried to destroy in someone else what you really did not like about yourself?

_____

_____

_____

_____

_____

_____

_____

_____

_____

You hypocrite, first cast the beam out of your own eye; and then you shall see clearly to cast the mote out of your brother's eye.
(Matthew 7:5)

If you want to change the world, a good place to start is with yourself. This statement may suggest that once we clean up our own act, we will be qualified to begin cleaning up the acts of others. I suspect the wisdom here is a bit more complicated than that. Many are sure to discover that cleaning up our own act is too much of a full-time job to then worry about others.

What have you done lately to remove the beams from your eyes?

_____

_____

_____

_____

_____

_____

_____

_____

_____

Give not that which is holy to dogs, neither cast your pearls
before swine, lest they trample them under their feet,
and turn again and rend you. (Matthew 7:6)

It is as ridiculous to profane what is sacred as it is to waste what is precious. Be prudent in dispensing the priceless treasure you have received. What is holy cannot be appreciated by people who have no sense of the sacred, just as precious things are not valued by those who do not sense their worth. Be careful to share what is holy with those who will respect the sanctity of the divine and to share what is precious with those who understand its importance.

What can you do to keep from sharing what is sacred with those who will profane it and from sharing what is precious with those who won't appreciate it?

Ask, and it shall be given you; seek, and you shall find;
knock, and it shall be opened unto you: For everyone
that asks receives; and he that seeks finds; and to him
that knocks it shall be opened. (Matthew 7:7-8)

Here is a promise attached to a threefold duty. There is something that you must do. Ask, seek, and knock. Inquire, pursue, and touch. Make inquiry about your life. Pursue the purpose of your life. Touch with certainty the possibility for your life. God is there to provide answers to all three.

In what way can you begin to ask questions about your life as you seek purpose in order to fulfill the possibility of your life?

_____

_____

_____

_____

_____

_____

_____

_____

_____

Or what man is there of you, whom if his son ask for bread,
will he give him a stone? Or if he ask a fish, will he
give him a serpent? (Matthew 7:9-10)

Like a loving parent, God provides for what we need. Think how
a loving, caring guardian responds to the request of a child for
food! The guardian fulfills the request gladly. God responds in like
manner to those who ask to be given what is so necessary as they
are driven to achieve that for which they strive.

What story from your life illustrates how God has provided for
you as a loving guardian supplies a child's needs?

_____

_____

_____

_____

_____

_____

_____

_____

If you then, being evil, know how to give good gifts unto your children, how much more shall your Father which is in heaven give good things to them that ask him? (Matthew 7:11)

As unruly as we are, we know how to give a good gift to those who ask us. How then can we doubt God's inherent goodness in providing for our needs? As a loving, caring parent is pleased to answer the child's request positively, so God delights to answer those who call on him graciously.

What does it take for you to be convinced that God responds to your situation in the most loving and perfect way?

_____

_____

_____

_____

_____

_____

_____

_____

_____

Therefore all things whatsoever you would that people do to you,
do you even so to them: for this is the law and the prophets.
(Matthew 7:12)

This well-known axiom—the Golden Rule—applies a basic principle for human interaction. Treat people as you want to be treated. What better rule or principle of practice could anyone give than this one?

How can you practice this principle in your relationships with others?

_____

_____

_____

_____

_____

_____

_____

_____

_____

_____

Enter you in at the strait gate: for wide is the gate, and broad is the way, that leads to destruction, and many there be which go in thereat. (Matthew 7:13)

"Everybody is doing it" is the phrase of youthful submission to joining the crowd. But young people are not alone in going along to get along just because we want to belong. Here is a general caution: Find the way that makes life more than just going along. The road less traveled is the one that calls those who would be true to a different cause.

How can you begin to make a different choice that can lead you away from the crowd to a better course?

_____

_____

_____

_____

_____

_____

_____

_____

_____

Because strait is the gate, and narrow is the way, which leads to life, and few there be that find it. (Matthew 7:14)

Frightening truth raises our level of consciousness concerning the way we are going and what we are doing with our lives. The way to life is straight and narrow and seldom cluttered. If you only seek safety in numbers, you just get lost in the pack, mimicking others. Maybe the path with just a few travelers is the best place in the world from which to view the road you ought to be taking. It is easier to see when the crowd is thin whom to follow.

In what way can you take the road less traveled to achieve a fuller life in Christ?

_____

_____

_____

_____

_____

_____

_____

_____

_____

_____

*Beware of false prophets, which come to you in sheep's clothing,
but inwardly they are ravening wolves.* (Matthew 7:15)

Here is a remarkable warning concerning false representation.
There are those who pretend to be what they are not and cause
great harm by distorting reality. We are called to wisdom. We are
called to compare the words and teaching of self-proclaimed
prophets with the words and principles of Christ. In doing so, we
will be equipped to discern the hearts of those who would desire to
claim our allegiance.

How can being more discerning about those who teach you help
you in your spiritual growth?

_____

_____

_____

_____

_____

_____

_____

_____

_____

_____

You shall know them by their fruits. Do men gather grapes of thorns, or figs of thistles? (Matthew 7:16)

The best test of what one believes is how his or her life is ordered by what he or she receives. The crop that is grown comes from the seed that is sown. The produce will make known exactly what has been going on. Check to see the crop before you decide to give your allegiance to those who may not be as godly as they pretend.

What kind of produce should you see before you make a commitment to follow someone?

_____

_____

_____

_____

_____

_____

_____

_____

_____

_____

Even so every good tree brings forth good fruit; but a corrupt tree brings forth evil fruit. (Matthew 7:17)

We've all heard the saying, "The fruit does not fall far from the tree." We bear what is in us as we continue to grow, and the harvest that we produce will let everyone know whether or not we are real or fake.

How can you confirm the authenticity of what you are being taught?

_____

_____

_____

_____

_____

_____

_____

_____

_____

_____

_____

A good tree cannot bring forth evil fruit, neither can a corrupt
tree bring forth good fruit. (Matthew 7:18)

Have you ever noticed that the description of an act and the way
you refer to the person who does the act contain the same word for
the act? A person who cheats is a cheater. A person who lies is a
liar. You get the point, I am sure. People are known by what they
do. And in doing they reveal to us all how they should be labeled,
whether good or corrupt.

In what way is the legitimacy of a person made known?

_____

_____

_____

_____

_____

_____

_____

_____

_____

_____

Every tree that does not bring forth good fruit is hewn down,
and cast into the fire. (Matthew 7:19)

God designed nature such that it destroys what is unproductive. Whatever fails to serve its purpose becomes useless and worthless. These words are a warning to us. God is a loving God, as we see time and again from Jesus' words. But God has no use for trees that are not bearing fruit. Neither should we be satisfied until we are fulfilling the purposes for which we were created.

What are you doing to make sure that the trees of your spiritual growth are bearing fruit?

_____

_____

_____

_____

_____

_____

_____

_____

_____

> *Wherefore by their fruits you shall know them.*
> (Matthew 7:20)

You are known by what you produce. The best way to determine what anyone is like is to see what his or her life generates. We do tend to replicate who we are as we reproduce what we are. Bear in mind that what you do speaks volumes about you.

Given the fruit you produce, what do you think people would say about you?

_____

_____

_____

_____

_____

_____

_____

_____

_____

_____

_____

_____

> *Not everyone that says unto me, Lord, Lord, shall enter into the kingdom of heaven; but he or she that does the will of my Father which is in heaven.* (Matthew 7:21)

The proof of faithfulness to Christ is obedience to the will of God. God's will is identical to what is good for humanity, as what is good for humanity is one and the same with the will of God. The two are synonymous, both revealing the same thing. The two are reflective of one another. God wills only what is in the best interest of people.

What would it take for you to embrace the will of God fully as the pattern by which you govern your life?

_____

_____

_____

_____

_____

_____

_____

_____

_____

_____

> *Many will say to me in that day, Lord, Lord, have we not prophesied in your name? and in your name cast out devils? and in your name done many wonderful works? And then I will profess unto them, I never knew you: depart from me, you that work iniquity.* (Matthew 7:22-23)

There is no substitute for authenticity. Imagine spending your energy and time doing something only to be told that it reeks of insincerity. There is nothing worse than being told that you are a fake. That is probably the worst comment anyone can make. Be sure that you are real as you give yourself to God.

How would you validate your sincerity as a disciple of Christ?

_____

_____

_____

_____

_____

_____

_____

_____

_____

_____

Therefore whosoever hears these sayings of mine, and does them,
I will liken him unto a wise man, which built his house upon a
rock: And the rain descended, and the floods came, and the
winds blew, and beat upon that house; and it fell not: for it was
founded upon a rock. (Matthew 7:24-25)

The Lord's teachings demand a decision. The choice is between either hearing and doing or hearing and ignoring what's been heard. The best advice in the world is of little consequence if it is not acted upon with confidence. Those who hear and believe are considered wise like those who build on a solid foundation. Don't let the best advice in the world escape you because you refuse to do what it says.

In what way can you be more diligent in building your life on the solid foundation of the Word of God?

_____

_____

_____

_____

_____

_____

_____

And everyone that hears these sayings of mine, and does not do
them, shall be likened unto a foolish man, which built his house
upon the sand: And the rain descended, and the floods came,
and the winds blew, and beat upon that house; and it fell:
and great was the fall of it. (Matthew 7:26-27)

To hear and fail to practice is considered foolish, like a person who builds on an unstable foundation. Imagine knowing what you need to do and still refusing to do it. What an awful fate awaits those who know what to do but decide not to do. The life you build crumbles because it is built on faults.

How can you avoid having your life disintegrate when faced with the variety of changes that will inevitably occur?

_____

_____

_____

_____

_____

_____

_____

_____

I will: be thou clean. (Luke 5:13)

In your distress, make your desire known to the Lord in faith with the assurance that the Lord will answer your call. The Lord's will is best for us regardless of what we face. The Lord's response to our condition is to will to cleanse us where we are so that we can live a better, more fulfilling life.

How does the Lord cleanse or purify your life to improve the quality of your life?

_____

_____

_____

_____

_____

_____

_____

_____

_____

Your sins are forgiven you. (Luke 5:20)

The burden and weight of our faults and failures exact quite a toll on our lives. Jesus alleviates the burden and lifts the weight by granting us forgiveness. We do not need to carry what we have been given permission to release. Let go of what retards your growth. You no longer need to let it make you languish.

What do you need to let go of as you accept the forgiveness Jesus has given you?

_____

_____

_____

_____

_____

_____

_____

_____

_____

_____

Follow me. (Luke 5:27)

In the routine activities of our lives, we hear the voice that gives us the opportunity to choose. The choice is there for you alone to make. You will not be forced, but only invited to consider the possibility of what can happen based on what you choose. Examine what you have done to get to where you are. And make a better choice, a choice to follow the Lord.

What is keeping you from responding positively to the invitation to follow Jesus?

_____

_____

_____

_____

_____

_____

_____

_____

_____

_____

What do you want me to do for you? (Mark 10:51)

Here is a question worth answering, particularly when you consider who is doing the asking. Take a moment and be clear what you would want the Lord to do for you. Do not miss the opportunity of a lifetime to get what can turn your life around. Consider carefully what prevents you from living life to the fullest before you ask for something that turns out to be foolish.

For what would you ask as you ponder this question today?

_____

_____

_____

_____

_____

_____

_____

_____

_____

_____

Go your way; your faith has made you whole. (Mark 10:52)

Faith is the channel by which the power of God can flow into our lives. It has been said, "If you have the faith, God has the power." Nothing moves the Lord like a person filled with faith. It is one of the few things at which the Lord marvels. Answer in faith the Lord's request and see what happens with your life.

How can you develop a faith that gets the Lord's attention?

_____

_____

_____

_____

_____

_____

_____

_____

_____

_____

_____

Go your way into the village over against you: and as soon as you have entered into it, you shall find a colt tied, whereon never a person sat; loose him, and bring him. (Mark 11:2)

The Lord makes requests of us and elicits our involvement in fulfilling what God is doing in the world. Whether it is to prepare for a sacred observance or the realization of a promise, God assigns and uses people as participants in the unfolding drama of life's varying scenarios. Everyone has a part to play and a role to assume to make the world a better place. Listen carefully at what you are being asked to do so that you, too, can be a part of the Lord's will.

How can you become a partner with what God is doing in the world?

My soul is exceeding sorrowful unto death: tarry you here,
and watch with me. (Matthew 26:38)

The Lord invites and involves us as participants in the pain and pathos that accompany the solitude, sacrifice, sorrow, and struggle of fulfilling one's purpose. We want to reign with the Lord, but we do not want to do what it takes. We cannot appreciate the power of the Lord's resurrection until we have accepted the reality of the Lord's suffering.

What does it mean for you to respond positively to the Lord's invitation to share in his suffering?

_____

_____

_____

_____

_____

_____

_____

_____

_____

O my Father, if it be possible, let this cup pass from me:
nevertheless, not as I will, but as thou wilt. (Matthew 26:39)

It is not always easy to admit that what we desire is not consistent
with God's will. Realizing that our personal desires pale in significance to fulfilling the will of God requires intense reflection and
honesty on our part. Subjecting ourselves to God's expectation
requires letting go of personal considerations and interests to honor
and follow the purpose of God, trusting that what God desires is
better than what we want.

In what way is what you desire inconsistent with what God
wills?

_____

_____

_____

_____

_____

_____

_____

_____

_____

Could you not watch with me one hour? (Matthew 26:40)

Regrettably, there are times when we disappoint the Lord with our failure to do what the Lord asks us to do. While the spirit is willing, the flesh is weak. We start out one way and end up another. We find ourselves with the best of intentions yet unable to achieve what we plan. Something gets in the way and prevents us from fulfilling our design.

In what way(s) have you failed to live up to what you said you would do?

_____

_____

_____

_____

_____

_____

_____

_____

_____

_____

He that dips his hand with me in the dish, the same shall betray me. (Matthew 26:23)

How penetrating and perturbing are these words in all of Scripture? They are a reminder of a reality we would prefer to forget. It is difficult for us to admit we have all done what betrays what the Lord expects. Often we who are the Lord's friends become the Lord's enemies. How tragic it is that friends can betray trust and take advantage of their place of privilege.

What have you done to betray the Lord instead being a faithful, trustworthy friend?

_____

_____

_____

_____

_____

_____

_____

_____

Father, forgive them; for they know not what they do.
(Luke 23:34)

One unfortunate reality about life is that so much of what we do is done in ignorance. We cause great harm unknowingly. We do not know what we are doing even though we think we do. Because God's activity is inconsistent with our desire, we try to force God to do what we want God to do. Know that the Lord forgives us for our lack of trust.

What have you done in ignorance for which you need the Lord's forgiveness?

_____

_____

_____

_____

_____

_____

_____

_____

_____

APRIL 17

Verily I say unto you, today shall you be with me in paradise.
(Luke 23:43)

In life's worst situations the Lord promises an outcome that reverses the effects of detrimental experiences. There is a future beyond what we see that is better than we can imagine. The Lord speaks a word of hope to help us get beyond the worst fate we can face. The Lord promises a future of personal existence in a place of beauty.

In what way has the Lord turned a negative result you brought on yourself into a positive outcome you never dreamed possible?

_____

_____

_____

_____

_____

_____

_____

_____

_____

_____

> *Be not afraid: go tell my brethren that they go into Galilee,
> and there they shall see me.* (Matthew 28:10)

In the ordinary, everyday scenes of our lives, the Lord's presence can be discerned, even though it may at times be disguised. The Lord meets us where we are to help us get to where we will be. That is the guarantee we have when the emptiness of loss attempts to render us helpless. Take a moment and look around; you too can hear the comforting sound that will settle your doubts and fears.

When have you been assured in the midst of fear that the Lord's direction was near?

_____

_____

_____

_____

_____

_____

_____

_____

> *Peace be unto you: as my Father has sent me,*
> *even so I send you.* (John 20:21)

Receiving the peace of the Lord and accepting the commission of the Lord seem to go hand in hand. You cannot have one without the other. They accompany each other "like birds of a feather." When you are given peace, you are then charged to carry what you have been given to those who will benefit from what you have experienced.

How can you accept the commission to make known the peace you have received from the Lord?

_____

_____

_____

_____

_____

_____

_____

_____

_____

> *Reach hither thy finger, and behold my hands;*
> *and reach hither thy hand, and thrust it into my side:*
> *and be not faithless but believing.* (John 20:27)

The Lord meets honest doubts with evidence that convinces, with the caveat that the questioner must take responsibility for interpreting what he senses. There is always proof for honest doubt. When you doubt the reality of the Lord's presence in your life because it seems that what you have heard is too good to be believed, the Lord will make available an opportunity for you to secure the validation you seek.

In what way has the evidence you require been provided for you to believe in what the Lord is doing in your life?

_____

_____

_____

_____

_____

_____

_____

_____

_____

Children, have you caught anything? (John 21:5)

The Lord is present to us during the difficult periods of adjustments in our lives. When we don't know what to do, we do what we have always done as a way of helping us get through what we are experiencing. In the midst of our attempts to manage what is simply overwhelming, we discover the expression of the care of the Lord. The Lord wants to know whether or not we are doing reasonably well with our attempts to manage what we are facing. The Lord's care is discovered in the expressed concern about our condition.

How have you experienced the care of the Lord during the difficult periods of adjustments in your life?

_____

_____

_____

_____

_____

_____

_____

_____

_____

_____

Cast the net on the right side of the ship, and you shall find.
(John 21:6)

The Lord provides a remedy for our failed efforts and gives us specific advice that alleviates our condition. We need to know what to do when the expenditure of our energy is an exercise in futility. There are times when we do all we know to do and still our situation does not change. The advice the Lord gives directs us to where what we seek is available. Follow the Lord's directives, and see if what you require is available to you as you adjust to the changes in your life.

In what way has the Lord's direction helped you find what you need during the changes in your life?

_____

_____

_____

_____

_____

_____

_____

_____

_____

Bring of the fish which you have now caught.
(John 21:10)

Compliance yields great benefits far beyond what you can imagine. So surrender to the One who deserves your allegiance. What you have been permitted to acquire is what the Lord uses to increase your awareness of God's activity in your life. Consider the abundance you have been permitted to catch as a result of doing what you were told to do.

How have you benefited from trusting the Lord's instructions?

_____

_____

_____

_____

_____

_____

_____

_____

_____

_____

_____

Simon, son of Jonas, do you love me more than these?
(John 21:15)

Love for the Lord is a prerequisite for faithful service. We do what we do because of our love for the person with whom we are in relationship. The Lord wants to know if we love him, because there will be no difficulty in our doing what the Lord requests if we love him. As a matter of fact, the test of the extent of our love for the Lord can be measured in how well we do what the Lord asks. Do you love the Lord more than anything or anyone?

How would you describe your willingness to do what the Lord asks of you?

_____

_____

_____

_____

_____

_____

_____

_____

All power is given unto me in heaven and in earth.
(Matthew 28:18)

We have all the backing we need to accomplish what we are being sent to do. How often do you really set out on a venture with that assurance? Authority as well as power backs the commission we receive. Authority is the capacity to command, and power is the ability to control. Go forward in the authority of the Lord's might to witness to the reality of the presence in whose name we live.

In what way can your life benefit from the awareness of the Lord's authority and power in your life?

_____

_____

_____

_____

_____

_____

_____

_____

> *Wait for the promise of the Father, which you have heard of me.* (Acts 1:4)

Our lives seem to revolve around waiting. We wait for just about everything. We wait for the fulfillment of a dream that has been deferred, the realization of long-anticipated hope, the right time, the right person. Waiting is a part of what we do. We are asked by the Lord to wait until we receive what will transform our lives and charge us with the power we need.

What keeps you from waiting for the fulfillment of what the Lord has promised?

_____

_____

_____

_____

_____

_____

_____

_____

_____

_____

For John truly baptized with water; but you shall be baptized
with the Holy Ghost not many days hence. (Acts 1:5)

In anticipation of something expected, we become as children in our excitement. Channel your energy and control your thoughts as you wait to be fulfilled by the Lord. You will be surprised at what you will receive when you open your heart to the Lord and believe. When you receive, do so knowing that you got the Lord's best.

What would it take for you to give the Lord an opportunity to fill you with power, to make of your life something new?

_____

_____

_____

_____

_____

_____

_____

_____

_____

_____

Receive the Holy Ghost. (John 20:22)

What you need to face each day, the Lord provides. You are simply asked to receive what the Lord supplies and then to trust that you need nothing more. We may think we need a lot, but in truth we need very little. We need only to receive the Holy Spirit, the presence of One who will never leave.

What keeps you from receiving what the Lord gives to sustain you throughout your life?

_____

_____

_____

_____

_____

_____

_____

_____

_____

_____

It is not for you to know the times or the seasons, which the
Father has put in his own power. (Acts 1:7)

It is easy to be preoccupied with what we do not know and then use it as an excuse. We continue to try to find out what is concealed from us. There are things that God keeps to God's self. That is God's prerogative. Why tread on that turf when we have so much else to worry about? Explore what you have been given with care. Cherish it, enjoy it, and use it. Quite frankly, that is more than we need to know to develop the discipline we need to grow.

In what way have you been preoccupied with what you do not know, using it as an excuse that prevents your faith from growing?

_____

_____

_____

_____

_____

_____

_____

_____

_____

_____

_____

> *But you shall receive power, after the Holy Ghost is come upon you: and you shall be witnesses unto me both in Jerusalem, and in all Judea, and in Samaria, and unto the uttermost part of the earth.* (Acts 1:8)

We need to be empowered to become what we can be. The gift of power that the Lord makes available to us gives us exactly what we need to become what the Lord intends. We are given the power to witness to the reality of the presence of the Lord in our lives. The Lord equips us to create the momentum necessary for others to come to know what we have discovered so that they too can join those who have known borne testimony to God's love and blessings.

How has the gift of the Holy Spirit equipped you to witness to the reality of God's presence in your life?

*Go you therefore, and teach all nations, baptizing them in
the name of the Father, and of the Son, and of the Holy
Ghost: Teaching them to observe all things whatsoever
I have commanded you: and, lo, I am with you always,
even unto the end of the world. Amen. (Matthew 28:19-20)*

Ponder for a moment why you do what you do and see if it is not
something that someone passed on to you. We are sent out to replicate our faith by passing on to others what we have received. The
value of our existence is determined by what lives on after we are
gone, not by how much we were able to accumulate on our own.
In just about every sphere of our lives we reproduce what we have
known. The sum total of our existence is made up of what we forward to others as an expression of what is important to us. As you
pass on what you have received from Christ, you have the assurance of an abiding and constant presence as a companion.

What are you passing on that will survive your earthly existence?

_____

_____

_____

_____

_____

_____

_____

What do you seek? (John 1:38)

We do a lot of searching, often ending our search without finding what satisfies. Answer the above question and you will find what's ultimately most important to you. If you seek Jesus, you will discover more than you thought possible from any other. Be drawn to Jesus—just for who Christ is—with the assurance that you will find what you need in him.

What causes you to seek the Lord? What do you seek?

Come and see. (John 1:39)

Some reality speaks for itself. Draw near to Jesus for yourself, and you will discover that he is in a class with no other. Come and see a person fully human and fully alive, brimming with the possibility of changing lives. Come and see the Lord for who the Lord is, for what the Lord has done, and for what the Lord has promised.

What would it take for you to come and see anew who the Lord is?

_____

_____

_____

_____

_____

_____

_____

_____

_____

_____

_____

You are Simon, son of Jona: you shall be called Cephas.
(John 1:42)

Where is the horizon between who you are and what you can become? While capacity is given, potential must be cultivated. We all need someone who can see beyond who we are in order for us to become what we can be. Jesus looks beyond our present, seeing our future possibilities. He takes us along the path to fulfill a noble destiny. Come to Jesus, and you will discover all of what your life can truly be.

What do you think are the possibilities resulting from your life in Christ?

_____

_____

_____

_____

_____

_____

_____

_____

> *Take these things hence; make not my Father's house a*
> *house of merchandise.* (John 2:16)

There comes a time when something that happens causes a response of righteous indignation. The person who is spiritually sensitive has a low tolerance for behavior that is abominable and morally reprehensible. Conduct that desecrates what is holy or that profanes what is sacred deserves to be met with a response that is equally expressive. Righteous indignation is the natural reaction to activity that is sacrilegious.

What causes you to become righteously indignant?

_____

_____

_____

_____

_____

_____

_____

_____

_____

_____

> *Verily, verily, I say unto you, except a man be born again,*
> *he cannot see the kingdom of God.* (John 3:3)

We must first conceive what we will ultimately come to believe. Certain realities cannot be seen or understood short of a personal transformation, a rebirth, a spiritual awakening, a conversion to Christ. Nurture the seed that Christ puts in you, the seed that allows you to proclaim that you have been born anew. Then watch your life change in every way.

In what way(s) have you been made new in Christ?

_____

_____

_____

_____

_____

_____

_____

_____

_____

_____

The wind blows where it wills, and you hear the sound of it, but cannot tell whence it comes, and whither it goes: so is every one that is born of the Spirit. (John 3:8)

The wind is invisible as well as inscrutable in its movement; however, we know the wind is real because we can see its effects. As the breath is the symbol of the unseen vital principle of existence, so is the Spirit the essence of the nature of life. Just like the wind, the unseen Spirit of God provides evidence of its existence in the affairs of humanity.

How have you experienced the Lord at work in your life?

_____

_____

_____

_____

_____

_____

_____

_____

_____

_____

Are you a master of Israel, and you do not know these things? (John 3:10)

Some understanding defies explanation; certain realities are better caught than taught. We can know ever so much and still it is not enough to fathom the complexities of life's mysteries. As we live, we catch hold of what we know to be. I am reminded of that old expression, "If it has to be explained, you would not understand, and if you understand, there is no need to explain."

What are a few of the experiences in your life when you caught rather than were taught what you came to know?

_____

_____

_____

_____

_____

_____

_____

_____

_____

*If I have told you earthly things, and you believe not, how shall
you believe if I tell you of heavenly things?* (John 3:12)

Understanding is a gradual process. It starts somewhere and takes
you someplace else. You move from the simple to the sublime,
from the earthly to the heavenly. Our experiences are nothing more
than a faint reflection that there is so much more in store. The Lord
wants to know what it takes to convince us of what we need to
make a difference in our lives.

What does it take for you to become convinced about the knowledge and understanding that Christ imparts?

_____

_____

_____

_____

_____

_____

_____

_____

_____

_____

> *For God so loved the world, that he gave his only*
> *begotten Son, that whosoever believes in him*
> *should not perish, but have everlasting life.* (John 3:16)

We have all attempted to define that ever-elusive, intangible reality we call love. We have abused it, misused it, distorted its meaning, confused it with lust and sentimentality, caricatured it to resemble our false notions, diluted it with magic, chivalry, hypocrisy, ambition, insanity, infatuation, and selfishness. The love that God defines is a love that gives the very best to do what is necessary to preserve us from the destruction we cause ourselves. The remedy for our condition of ruin is the love of God expressed in Christ. Now that is real love.

How has the love of God as expressed in Christ saved you from the destruction you have brought on yourself?

For God sent not his Son into the world to condemn the world; but that the world through him might be saved. (John 3:17)

The purpose of God's activity in the world through Christ is the preservation of life. To save us all from destruction is the aim of God's manifestation in Christ. Jesus is the Lord's solution for a world that has become unwound, unraveling at the seams, spiraling downward. Jesus is God's best effort to do effective damage control by reversing or putting destructive forces on hold.

How has God's love in Christ reversed the destructive situations in your life?

_____

_____

_____

_____

_____

_____

_____

_____

_____

He that believes on him is not condemned. (John 3:18)

Belief provides a privilege. The benefit of believing is approval instead of rejection. Our belief confirms our acceptance. Belief is our willingness to embrace exemption from the penalty our behavior has merited. How can anyone refuse such a generous offer to believe?

What does it take for you to believe completely in what God has done in Christ?

*But he that does not believe on him is condemned
already, because he has not believed in the name of
the only begotten Son of God.* (John 3:18)

Just as faith confirms, doubt condemns. Doubt is the culprit that
cheats you out of living a life of faith. Doubt is the foe that tells you
there is nothing more to life than what you can see. Doubt is the
nemesis that causes you to dismiss reality. It attempts to destroy
what you already know without providing an alternative. Doubt is
what causes you to dismiss reality that you ought to face. It has an
adverse impact, one that diminishes and limits life's possibilities.

How have you permitted doubt to have an adverse impact on
your life?

_____

_____

_____

_____

_____

_____

_____

_____

> *And this is the condemnation that light has come into
> the world, and people loved darkness rather than
> light, because their deeds were evil.* (John 3:19)

Light reveals, but the dark conceals. We prefer darkness over light when we want to conceal what we don't want others to find out. Under the cloak of darkness we can continue to do what we want. Once the light has come, we do not have an excuse to continue doing what we know we should not do, but often we continue to use doubt as a way to explain our rejection of the light.

How have you used doubt to continue in darkness because you weren't ready to accept what the light revealed?

_____

_____

_____

_____

_____

_____

_____

_____

_____

_____

*For every one that does evil hates light, neither comes to the light,
lest his [or her] deeds should be reproved.* (John 3:20)

Sometimes we become too accustomed to the shadows that hide
the patterns and practices of our lives. We do not want anything
that will expose the way we have been. We want to be left alone to
be the way we are, and we want to remain that way, for if our comfort zone is disturbed, we may have to change. In all honesty, when
challenged by light to change our lives, we would rather live in
darkness under the cover of night.

When have you rejected light because you were comfortable with
the darkness in your life?

_____

_____

_____

_____

_____

_____

_____

_____

_____

*But he that does truth comes to the light, that his deeds may be
made manifest, that they are wrought by God.* (John 3:21)

We cannot seem to come into the light on our own. We need prod-
ding. When we accept what God has done in Christ, there is a
surge that continues to flow through our lives, an energy that continues to grow, directing us toward God until at last we reflect in
our behavior the change that God can bring about in us.

In what way has the surge from the energy of what God has done
in Christ brought about needed changes in your life?

_____

_____

_____

_____

_____

_____

_____

_____

_____

_____

Give me to drink. (John 4:7)

The Lord puts himself in the position of being the recipient of our kind consideration and gracious generosity. Instead of our making a request of the Lord, here is an occasion for us to hear the Lord's appeal to us. Give me some of what you have come to get for yourself. We are always so consumed with what we want that we neglect to consider what the Lord wants of us. Pause for a moment to hear this request and then decide how you will answer.

How do you respond to the requests the Lord makes of you?

_____

_____

_____

_____

_____

_____

_____

_____

_____

_____

_____

*If you knew the gift of God, and who it is that says to you,
Give me to drink; you would have asked of him, and he
would have given you living water.* (John 4:10)

Think about how often we miss much of what the Lord could do
simply because we don't recognize God. It is frightening to think
that our responses to the Lord are sometimes more influenced by
our biases and lack of knowledge than by a generous, compassionate heart. Be awake. Be looking to encounter God in your living each day.

When have you missed an opportunity for living water because
you didn't recognize God?

_____

_____

_____

_____

_____

_____

_____

_____

_____

Whosoever drinks of this earthly water shall thirst again.
(John 4:13)

Nothing seems to satisfy us permanently. What we do get has to be replenished time and time again, for earthly desire can be only temporarily pleased before we have to return to get more of the same. The cycle continues to go on and on as long as we live. We get thirsty, we quench our thirst, and then we get thirsty again. We keep going round and round in a monotonous quest to get what will satiate our desire.

What do you have to do to satisfy the continual cravings of your life?

_____

_____

_____

_____

_____

_____

_____

_____

_____

_____

*But whosoever drinks of the water that I shall
give shall never thirst.* (John 4:14)

In a world where we are in constant pursuit because what we get
we need to replenish, the Lord promises perpetual fulfillment and
permanent satisfaction as a perennial reservoir gushing forth inces-
santly. What the Lord provides satisfies completely, consummately,
and continually. Imagine being fulfilled entirely, perfectly, and constantly. Now what more could anyone ask for?

How have you missed the opportunity of a lifetime to have nev-
er-ending fulfillment?

_____

_____

_____

_____

_____

_____

_____

_____

_____

> *But the water that I shall give shall be a well of water*
> *springing up to everlasting life.* (John 4:14)

Jesus Christ gives an ever-ready, inexhaustible, never failing, over-flowing supply that satisfies always. You don't have to go looking anywhere for what the Lord provides. It's living right there in your heart. The Lord has put it where you need it to be so that you can get to it anytime. Come and let the Lord give you your personal reservoir.

What keeps you from accepting the gift of this perpetual fulfillment?

_____

_____

_____

_____

_____

_____

_____

_____

_____

_____

> *Woman, believe me, the hour comes, when you shall neither in this mountain, nor yet in Jerusalem, worship the Father.*
> (John 4:21)

We do "make mountains out of molehills," as the old expression goes. That's another way of saying that we put too much emphasis on what is less important. We make what is minor major, neglecting to keep what is essential most important. The place of worship is not as important as the subject of our worship. My, how we permit what is secondary to eclipse what is primary.

How have you given the secondary primary emphasis in your life?

_____

_____

_____

_____

_____

_____

_____

_____

_____

_____

You worship you know not what.
(John 4:22)

How often are we ignorant of who we really worship? Sometimes we have an understanding of God that is not necessarily based on knowledge. We have accepted what we have been told was in vogue at the time. Now we find out through new information that what we have been told is not altogether accurate. Getting beyond what we have learned requires being willing to be taught again.

How can you correct your misconceptions about the God you worship?

_____

_____

_____

_____

_____

_____

_____

_____

_____

We know what we worship; for salvation is of the Jews.
(John 4:22)

Jesus knows God. The One who is closest to God, Jesus, provides our knowledge and understanding of God. Jesus speaks with authority because he is the expressed image of God as well as the perfect reflection of the will of God. Jesus is the clearest picture of what God is like. So we can trust what Jesus says about God.

How can you learn to trust more than any other image you have been given the picture of God Jesus presents?

_____

_____

_____

_____

_____

_____

_____

_____

_____

_____

> *But the hour comes, and now is, when the true worshippers*
> *shall worship the Father in spirit and in truth.* (John 4:23)

True worship consists of two basic elements: spirit, the essence of life, and truth, the facts about life. True worship begins in the heart as one seeks after God. First you acknowledge the basic nature of existence as spiritual. Then you accept the truth about life. Worship affirms what we cannot see so that we can understand more clearly what we do see. Spirit and truth go together; one speaks of essence and the other of substance.

In what way can you begin to worship based on the essence of God's nature?

_____

_____

_____

_____

_____

_____

_____

_____

_____

For the Father seeks such to worship him. (John 4:23)

The divine search is for those whose reverence is authentic. God is seeking those who truly know how to worship properly. The Lord is seeking those who want to come to him with true affection. Sad to say, often we come with a personal agenda to try to manipulate in order to control rather than approach the Lord with total adoration and humility.

What would you have to do to become the one the Lord is seeking?

_____

_____

_____

_____

_____

_____

_____

_____

_____

_____

God is a spirit. (John 4:24)

Jesus describes God in the fundamental essence of God's nature as free from all conditions of time and space. What a far-reaching, comprehensive description of the character of God this is. God is not circumscribed by the limits that keep us captive or restricted by the conditions of our lives. God is not defined by what is but defines all that is. God is totally free, not bound or controlled by anything. God is sovereign.

How can an appreciation of God as spirit expand and heighten your worship experience?

> *And they that worship him must worship him in*
> *spirit and in truth.* (John 4:24)

One of the facts of faith is that our actions are an echo of our attitude; our behavior is a reflection of our belief. Think about how you are and what that reveals about you. Think about what you do and what it says about you. The spirit captures the essence of who you are and the truth defines the way you are.

How can you improve the quality of your worship so that it is more consistent with what God desires?

_____

_____

_____

_____

_____

_____

_____

_____

_____

_____

_____

I that speak unto you am he. (John 4:26)

Too often we get stuck in certain patterns of thought all because of what we have been taught. We form strong opinions built on prejudice and thus run the risk of missing opportunities. God makes available to us the very chance we need to hear what will help to correct what has gone wrong. The Lord speaks through Christ with certainty to give us what we need to change our understanding so that our faith can become authentic and not just a replication of what we have been taught to mimic.

What would it take for you to get beyond your biases so that you can benefit from what it means to hear Jesus' voice and embrace Jesus fully?

_____

_____

_____

_____

_____

_____

_____

_____

_____

I have meat to eat that you know not of. (John 4:32)

There is a satisfaction that dwarfs hunger or craving of any kind in fulfilling a higher purpose. To be consumed by what you are doing to the extent that you forget about everything else, particularly your own desires, is what happens when you are compelled to pursue God's purposes. The thrill of it all diminishes everything so that you are full enough with what you are doing.

In what ways have you been so consumed with fulfilling a purpose that no other craving or desire seemed to matter?

> *My meat is to do the will of him that sent me, and to finish his work.* (John 4:34)

The business of life that claims our attention is larger than we know; it encompasses so much more than we realize. There is something going on of which we are a part, whether we realize it or not. True satisfaction comes from knowing that you are fulfilling your purpose for being. Doing your part in the scheme of things yields rewards that are thoroughly fulfilling.

In what way has fulfilling your purpose fed and nourished you through life?

_____

_____

_____

_____

_____

_____

_____

_____

_____

Say not you, there are yet four months, and then comes the harvest? Behold, I say unto you, Lift up your eyes, and look on the fields; for they are white already to harvest. (John 4:35)

Jesus perceives what we often miss. People are ready, like crops, to be harvested so that their lives can produce something useful. All they need is to have their awareness about their capacity heightened so that they can become excited about fulfilling their potential. We are encouraged to be the ones who will go and gather those who are waiting.

In what way can you become one who reaps for Christ?

_____

_____

_____

_____

_____

_____

_____

_____

_____

_____

> *And one that reaps receives wages, and gathers*
> *fruit unto life eternal.* (John 4:36)

"It pays to serve Jesus" is the way one composer put it in a song. No work for the Lord is in vain. Serving Christ yields benefits for all believers. There is fruit that is born from every effort, fruit that accrues to your account. The pay you receive is much more than you can ever consider, for it extends without limit, continually producing a return. Now that is an investment worth making, one that produces both generously and continuously.

How would you describe the benefit you receive as a reaper for the Lord?

_____

_____

_____

_____

_____

_____

_____

_____

_____

_____

That both he that sows and he that reaps
may rejoice together. (John 4:36)

Everyone benefits in the harvest process: the one who sows and the
one who reaps. Both have a part to play. They are dependent on
each other. One plants; the other gathers. Without one you would
not have a crop, and without the other you would not have a gathered yield. Both are necessary for the process to be complete. In the
end they rejoice together.

How do you contribute to the process of sowing and reaping so
that you join the rejoicing in the end?

_____

_____

_____

_____

_____

_____

_____

_____

And herein is that saying true, one
sows, and another reaps.
(John 4:37)

To some this saying has become a cliché. Clichés remind us of reality we are prone to ignore or in some instances forget. Many observations in life serve as constant reminders of what we already know to be true. We can grow so accustomed to seeing them that they lose the reality of their truth. Sometimes a gentle nudge with a lesson about life can bring to memory what we have forgotten.

What does it take for you to be reminded about reality you are prone to ignore or forget?

_____

_____

_____

_____

_____

_____

_____

_____

_____

> *I sent you to reap that whereon you bestowed*
> *not labor: other men labored, and you are*
> *entered into their labors.* (John 4:38)

Life is an interlocking network of dependencies that build on themselves and provide for everyone an opportunity to pick up where others have left off. In other words, you get a head start because you are standing as it were on the shoulders of those who have gone before. We have benefited from untold persons who have preceded us. Time would not permit us to list all of those who have contributed to what we have achieved. The truth, however, is that we have received from them great benefit. We inherit what others have sown as others reap the results of our growth.

How have you benefited as a result of the efforts of others? How have others benefited from your efforts?

_____

_____

_____

_____

_____

_____

_____

_____

_____

_____

_____

_____

Except you see signs and wonders, you will not believe.
(John 4:48)

Here is an observation about a widespread element of human nature. Too often we require amazing, extraordinary evidence of God's greatness. We expect God to prove himself over and over again. Regrettably, even upon seeing what we ask to see we still don't believe. Have you ever noticed that sometimes whatever you do, it isn't enough to convince people?

What did it take or what does it take for you to believe in Jesus?

_____

_____

_____

_____

_____

_____

_____

_____

_____

_____

Go your way; your son lives. (John 4:50)

The answer that Christ gives to our desperate plea is one that satisfies the concern that brings us to him. We are usually brought closer to the Lord by some circumstance that holds us captive. It may be that someone we love needs what only the Lord can give, so we come begging and pleading to get our hopes fulfilled. How gracious it is of the Lord to meet our need. He did so then, and he does so now.

In what ways has the Lord remedied your life's ills?

Will you be made whole? (John 5:6)

The answer to life's vital concerns can be found in our responses to the questions the Lord asks. The Lord causes us to consider what we really want by making an inquiry that requires that we take an honest look at ourselves. We find ourselves in our spiritual impotence in a place where we can feel empowered watching others get what we desire. Jesus reorders our priorities by focusing on what should be the main object of our desires: wholeness.

What is your true desire?

_____

_____

_____

_____

_____

_____

_____

_____

_____

Rise, take up your bed and walk. (John 5:8)

Jesus cuts through the excuses we make by telling us what it takes for us to have the life we desire. The Lord empowers us to take responsibility for our lives. We cannot sit idly, waiting superstitiously for something magical to happen. Get up and do something about bringing to pass what you want to see. Don't make excuses. Get up and walk.

In what way do you need to be empowered by Christ to take responsibility for your life?

_____

_____

_____

_____

_____

_____

_____

_____

_____

_____

Behold, you are made whole. (John 5:14)

Jesus empowers you to get up from where you are so that you can make the most of your life. Once you follow the Lord's command, you find you have the courage not just to stand, but to walk. Once on your feet, go to a sacred place where you can at least thank God for the change in your life. The change in your life will be confirmed.

What positive change has the Lord confirmed in your life?

_____

_____

_____

_____

_____

_____

_____

_____

_____

_____

> *Sin no more, lest a worse thing come unto you.*
> (John 5:14)

When our suffering has been brought to an end, we run the risk of going back to where it all began. Something in us seems to be drawn to the very thing that has caused us harm. So the Lord gives this word of caution. Be careful that you do not return to what caused you to be impaired in the first place, for if you do, this time it will be worse than before.

In what ways are you drawn to what impairs your quality of life?

_____

_____

_____

_____

_____

_____

_____

_____

_____

My Father works hitherto, and I work. (John 5:17)

The assurance we have about God's presence in our lives is the positive effect of what Christ accomplishes. Just like the proof of the pudding is in the tasting, so the evidence of the Lord's activity is in the result. Look how much better the world is as a result of the life of Jesus. Think about how much you, too, have benefited from the presence of the Lord in Christ.

In what way has the Lord's presence been confirmed in your life through Christ Jesus?

_____

_____

_____

_____

_____

_____

_____

_____

_____

_____

_____

JUNE 13 ❧

> *Verily, verily, I say unto you, The Son can do nothing*
> *of himself, but what he sees the Father do.*
> (John 5:19)

Jesus echoes the activity of God with his life. What Jesus does is synonymous with what God does. The two are one and the same. In Christ is the perfect reflection of the nature of God. God can be seen clearly in Christ. We likewise become godly ambassadors as we study the words and follow the advice of Jesus. Jesus points the way to the Triune God.

What picture of God comes to your mind when you consider Christ?

_____

_____

_____

_____

_____

_____

_____

_____

_____

> *For whatever the Father does, the Son does.*
> (John 5:19)

The Lord finds expression in definitive ways in Jesus. If you want to know what God does, look at what Jesus does. Jesus mirrors perfectly the heart, mind, and will of God. What you see in one is nothing more than a reflection of both.

How would you describe God by the activity of Christ?

_____

_____

_____

_____

_____

_____

_____

_____

_____

_____

> *For the Father loves the Son, and shows him*
> *all things that he does.* (John 5:20)

Jesus has a position of privilege by virtue of his unique relationship with God. Jesus knows more about God than we do. So Jesus is informed about matters on which others can only speculate. Since Jesus is in a better position to know, it seems reasonable that we will trust him to tell us and to show us the right way.

How have the words of Jesus pointed you toward God?

_____

_____

_____

_____

_____

_____

_____

_____

_____

_____

_____

_____

> *And he will show him greater works than these,*
> *that you may marvel.* (John 5:20)

Exclusive relationships provide special privileges. The unique connection of Jesus to God puts him in a position all by himself. God does through Christ what God does through no one else. God gets our attention in Christ by doing what causes us to be amazed.

How have you been amazed by what God has done in Christ?

_____

_____

_____

_____

_____

_____

_____

_____

_____

_____

> *For as the Father raises up the dead, and quickens them;*
> *even so the Son quickens whom he will.* (John 5:21)

No one can make the claim that God makes in Christ. Jesus has the power to give life. You can find in him all that you need to live. He adds to our existence what only he can give: life with all its grandeur and promise and meaning.

In what ways has Christ Jesus given you life?

_____

_____

_____

_____

_____

_____

_____

_____

_____

_____

_____

> *For the Father judges no one, but has committed*
> *all judgment to the Son.* (John 5:22)

All authority to determine the legitimacy of faith has been given to Jesus. Jesus measures the authenticity of faith. Jesus verifies the sincerity of our faith. Faithful existence in the world is evaluated by the example of Christ, for we all are intended to fulfill a purpose that transcends our lives.

How do you think Jesus would evaluate the sincerity of your faith?

_____

_____

_____

_____

_____

_____

_____

_____

_____

_____

> *That all people should honor the Son, even*
> *as they honor the Father.* (John 5:23)

God has set Christ forth as the expression of what God is like as well as what our possibility is in him. We get a twofold picture in Christ. On the one hand, we see God. On the other hand, we see our potential. In honoring Jesus you honor God. As God is worthy of honor, so is Christ.

What is the best way for you to honor Christ today as an expression of your honoring God?

_____

_____

_____

_____

_____

_____

_____

_____

_____

_____

> *He that honors not the Son honors not the*
> *Father who sent him.* (John 5:23)

Rejecting the one God sends is the same as rejecting God. You don't refuse anything from one whom you revere. You accept what is offered graciously, as the precious gift it is. Reverence and respect for one automatically translates into respect for what that one has offered to us as a priceless gift.

In what way do you understand that disrespecting Jesus is disregarding God?

_____

_____

_____

_____

_____

_____

_____

_____

_____

_____

_____

Verily, verily, I say unto you, He that hears my word, and believes on him that sent me, has everlasting life, and shall not come into condemnation; but is passed from death to life. (John 5:24)

Belief in Jesus affords us the privilege of getting beyond what threatens our existence. With his life Jesus showed us how to transcend whatever imperils our lives. It doesn't matter who or what it is, whether people or predicaments. With Christ you can accomplish what life has in store for you. This is the life beyond that Christ offers you.

What do you need to get beyond to get to the life that Christ has for you?

_____

_____

_____

_____

_____

_____

_____

_____

_____

_____

Verily, verily, I say to you, the hour is coming, and now is, when
the dead shall hear the voice of the Son of God: and they that
hear shall live. (John 5:25)

How often we fail to hear what will benefit us greatly. We are deaf
and dead to the voice that can bring about the best for our lives.
What Jesus says gives life. Hear what he says so that you can have
the life that accompanies believing in him. Listen and live.

What keeps you from hearing what Jesus says?

_____

_____

_____

_____

_____

_____

_____

_____

_____

_____

> *For as the Father has life in himself; so has he given*
> *to the Son to have life in himself.* (John 5:26)

Jesus possesses what he imparts: life. Come and receive what only he can give. The life you need and the hope to live productively may be found in him. Jesus gives the direction you require to get from here to there as well as all that goes with making a life of significance.

What would it take for you to embrace the life of significance Jesus offers us?

_____

_____

_____

_____

_____

_____

_____

_____

_____

_____

> *And has given him authority to execute judgment*
> *also, because he is the Son of man.* (John 5:27)

All the authority that is necessary to accomplish his purpose Jesus possesses in full measure. Jesus has this authority because he has already experienced what we experience. He has endured what we endure. He has faced what we face in life. Jesus understands us fully because he is one of us. He understands what goes on in us, with us, through us, and to us.

In what ways has Jesus associated himself with the human predicament?

_____

_____

_____

_____

_____

_____

_____

_____

_____

_____

Marvel not at this: for the hour is coming, in which all that are in the graves shall hear his voice. (John 5:28)

Even death does not exempt us from hearing what Christ says. What may seem incredible now will one day reveal the amazing power and authority of the Lord. For even when our life as we know it comes to an end, we will still hear what the Lord says about the life we have lived.

What would you want to hear the Lord say to you about your life when it ends?

_____

_____

_____

_____

_____

_____

_____

_____

_____

_____

> *And shall come forth; they that have done good, unto*
> *the resurrection of life; and they that have done evil, unto*
> *the resurrection of damnation.* (John 5:29)

There is a reward/recompense feature built into existence. There is no way to avoid facing what our choices bring to us as consequences. We may think that we can escape, but there is no way around getting what we earn. We will all be paid in the end. Make up your mind to please God and receive a reward that continues life. The other choice is to displease God and get the recompense your disregard carries with it. The choice is up to you.

What can you do to receive a reward that continues life?

_____

_____

_____

_____

_____

_____

_____

_____

_____

> *I can of my own self do nothing: as I hear, I judge: and my judgment is just; because I seek not my own will, but the will of the Father who has sent me.* (John 5:30)

Jesus said no to what he had a right to say yes to, and he said yes to what he had a right to say no to. He was willing to forego certain privileges to which he was entitled in order to accomplish something far more extraordinary. He was willing to subdue his personal ambitions and passions in order to realize a more noble purpose. We can see ourselves as Christ saw himself, one who was sent rather than one who just went. We are on a mission with a purpose to fulfill God's intent for creation.

In what way do you need to say no to what you have a right to say yes to or yes to what you have a right to say no to in order to fulfill the will of God?

_____

_____

_____

_____

_____

_____

_____

If I bear witness of myself, my witness is not true. (John 5:31)

A person's testimony of himself or herself is suspicious. Jesus' life and activity are reflections of God's intent for humanity and creation. God's purpose is mirrored in the life of Christ. What Jesus did reflected perfectly the will of God so that his personal desires were subjected to fulfilling a larger purpose. That purpose was to demonstrate what is in the best interest of preserving humanity. No sacrifice was too great, no surrender too small to effect what would be of benefit to all.

What sacrifices do you need to make to fulfill the larger purpose of God?

There is another that bears witness of me; and I know that the
witness which he witnesses of me is true. (John 5:32)

We all have a natural tendency to draw attention to ourselves and away from others. It takes courage as well as confidence to direct people to someone other than yourself. John the Baptist bears witness of Jesus rather than himself. Here is a clear example of one who is confident in himself and certain of his role as a believer. When we know our purpose, it is easier to accept our place.

In what way do you need to be more confident about yourself and more certain about your role as a believer?

_____

_____

_____

_____

_____

_____

_____

_____

_____

You sent unto John, and he bore witness to the truth.
(John 5:33)

Those who precede us prepare the way and provide direction for us. They make us aware of what we would miss otherwise. Like John, you can provide the direction someone may need to find in Jesus a better life. Learn how to tell others what you have come to know about what God has done in Christ so that others can benefit from your faith in him. After all, you did not receive faith to keep it to yourself, but to pass faith on to others who also need it.

How can you become like John, an effective witness who points others to Christ?

_____

_____

_____

_____

_____

_____

_____

_____

_____

_____

But I received not testimony from people: but these things I say, that you might be saved. (John 5:34)

Witnesses serve to convince those who need their testimony in order to believe. People listen to trustworthy witnesses. Those who are undeniably credible and reliable provide undisputed proof that is considered dependable. Are you the kind of witness to whom the Lord can refer someone?

What would it take for you to become that kind of witness?

_____

_____

_____

_____

_____

_____

_____

_____

_____

> *He was a burning and shining light, and you were willing*
> *for a season to rejoice in his light.* (John 5:35)

What a marvelous tribute Jesus pays John! He refers to John as a faithful believer who attracts others with his radiance and inviting glow. Those who see his brilliance cannot help but rejoice in his light. Imagine someone rejoicing for a season in the light of your life as your witness points them toward Christ.

What would it take for people to rejoice in the light of your life witnessing to Christ?

_____

_____

_____

_____

_____

_____

_____

_____

_____

_____

> *But I have greater witness than that of John: for the*
> *works which the Father has given me to finish, the*
> *same works that I do, bear witness of me, t*
> *hat the Father has sent me.* (John 5:36)

We do well to be reminded that Jesus' works speak for themselves. Some things do not need an explanation or even confirmation by anyone because what is done says it all. All that Jesus did in the course of his life depicted the reality of God's presence. Jesus came from God to accomplish the purpose of God for humanity. His deeds unequivocally speak to that.

How can the greater witness in the life of Christ confirm for you that Jesus has done the work of God?

_____

_____

_____

_____

_____

_____

_____

_____

_____

*And the Father himself, which has sent me, has borne
witness of me. You have neither heard his voice
at any time, nor seen his shape. (John 5:37)*

God bears witness of God's own. Sufficient evidence is provided of
who is sent. You will not be able to accomplish what is intended
unless God is at work in and through you. This is the assurance
Jesus gives. This is the faith that we confess.

In what ways has God particularly borne witness of Christ in
your life?

_____

_____

_____

_____

_____

_____

_____

_____

_____

_____

*And you have not his word abiding in you: for whom
he has sent, him you believe not.* (John 5:38)

It has been said that it doesn't matter what you believe, as long as
you believe something. That is a ridiculous statement! What you
believe makes all the difference in the world! If you believe God
was in Christ, then you will accept what God has done through
him. If you "believe not," you will not know God's work.

What has convinced you that God was in Christ doing something unique in the world?

_____

_____

_____

_____

_____

_____

_____

_____

_____

_____

Search the scriptures; for in them you think you have eternal life: and they are they which testify of me. (John 5:39)

We are so easily prone to misplace our trust by putting our confidence in the wrong things. Words are just that until they are fulfilled, until someone makes them become real. That is what Jesus does: with what we know of sacred Writ, he makes the words live rather than stay on the pages like a script.

How has Jesus brought to life the sacred Writ for you?

_____

_____

_____

_____

_____

_____

_____

_____

_____

_____

JULY 7 🌿

And you will not come to me, that you might have life.
(John 5:40)

Missed opportunities and neglected moments seem to catch every-one by surprise at one time or another. We fail to see what is avail-able because we cannot accept the way the possibility came to us. We reject what we want when it does not occur the way we think it should. It is a terrible tragedy to miss the one thing most needed to live.

In what ways have you refused to accept the life Jesus offers, because its arrival was not consistent with your point of view?

_____

_____

_____

_____

_____

_____

_____

_____

I receive not honor from people. (John 5:41)

Jesus did not court or covet the applause of people or seek the earthly pomp and splendor of the traditional thinking about his life. He was firmly rooted in an understanding of God's intention for his life and fully identified with God's grand design for him. Oh, to be secure in who you are, so that you refuse to be manipulated into what you are not!

In what ways can you fulfill God's purpose in your life, even if others do not give the confirmation you would like?

_____

_____

_____

_____

_____

_____

_____

_____

_____

_____

> *But I know you, that you have not the love of*
> *God in you.* (John 5:42)

It has been said that "love is as love does." Actions speak louder than words. The love of God is expressed in God-honoring ways. Something that dishonors God is not of God, for that would not be loving. Slighting what is truly of God also dishonors God. If we love God, we accept what God does and honor God with the love we then express.

How do you demonstrate that the love of God is in you?

_____

_____

_____

_____

_____

_____

_____

_____

_____

_____

_____

> *I am come in my Father's name, and you receive*
> *me not: if another shall come in his own name,*
> *you will receive him.* (John 5:43)

We often make our choices strangely. We choose according to the comfort we get, rather than receiving the disclosure that may change everything. We try hard to keep things as they are, not letting anyone rock our little boat, altering our plan. It is easier to choose less challenging options than what is best, for we really want a smooth, stress-free life. God comes in Christ to challenge us to choose differently so that we can be true to the image of God in whose likeness we are made.

What are some ways you confuse those who come in Jesus' name with those who come in their own name?

How can you believe, which receive honor one of another, and seek not the honor that comes from God only? (John 5:44)

When we seek the admiration of others, we run the risk of deluding ourselves about our druthers. We say we want the honor that comes from God, yet everything we do is meant to please those we know. If we keep in mind that self-delusion from desiring others to admire us often leads to big trouble, we won't be duped by what others give, for only what God offers will bring true life and honor.

How have you been deluded by wanting honor from people, rather than receiving honor that comes from God alone?

_____

_____

_____

_____

_____

_____

_____

_____

_____

Do not think that I will accuse you to the Father: there is one that accuses you, even Moses, in whom you trust. (John 5:45)

Our own faith accuses us when we inappropriately understand what we believe. Belief is not static but dynamic, always growing and reshaping our understanding. Unfortunately, faith is sometimes reduced to a means to control as opposed to being an opportunity to challenge people to stretch beyond the limits that confine life. Jesus challenges us to go where we have not gone before in our thinking about what God is doing as well as what God can do with our lives.

How have you inappropriately understood what you believe about God?

_____

_____

_____

_____

_____

_____

_____

_____

_____

JULY 13 🌿

> *For if you had believed Moses, you would have*
> *believed me: for he wrote of me.* (John 5:46)

It is something when the basis of our faith establishes the reality we deny. How often is that the case simply because we are not as conversant with what we say we believe as we pretend to be? We know bits and pieces, a little of this and a little of that. We need to interpret and understand with wider margins that allow and encourage us to grow beyond the boundaries of our limitations.

How have the restrictions of your interpretations limited you from growing beyond the narrowly defined boundaries of your understanding?

_____

_____

_____

_____

_____

_____

_____

_____

_____

> *But if you believe not his writings, how shall you*
> *believe my words?* (John 5:47)

We miss the deeper meaning and truth of what we say we believe when we close our minds to interpretations that could free us from the narrow confines of our limitations. Rather than distorting faith, new information expands our perception so that we can gain a more complete understanding. Integrating old and new understanding brings a better grasp of the truth.

How can you integrate what you know from the past and the present so that you can continue to grow your faith?

_____

_____

_____

_____

_____

_____

_____

_____

_____

It is I; be not afraid. (John 6:20)

The unexpected happens unannounced and brings into our lives so much doubt. Uncertainty accents our fear even though the Lord is near. We become afraid, for we are not exactly certain what lies ahead. Jesus alleviates our fears in the midst of our fright with words of comfort that bring great delight. "Be not afraid, for I am here." That settles our doubts and calms our fears.

What fears are put to rest for you by these comforting words of Jesus?

_____

_____

_____

_____

_____

_____

_____

_____

_____

_____

Verily, verily, I say unto you, you seek me, not because
you saw the miracles, but because you did eat
the loaves, and were filled. (John 6:26)

Sad but true that many follow Jesus for what they can get. They come to him for loaves instead of love. What does it take to appreciate Christ for who he is and not necessarily for what he can do? He longs especially to make us more aware of who he is. The ultimate goal of faith is to ignite love for the Lord in the heart of the believer. We will follow him because we love him. Ponder the motivation that draws you to Christ.

What is the attraction of Christ for you?

_____

_____

_____

_____

_____

_____

_____

_____

_____

Labor not for the meat which perishes, but for the meat which endures unto everlasting life, which the Son of man shall give unto you: for God the Father has sealed him. (John 6:27)

We spend our energy and time on what we will not be able to keep. Whatever we acquire in life will either leave us or we will leave it. You will not be able to keep any of it. So why spend all your energy to get what you can't keep? In Christ you can have what lasts forever: life beyond what threatens your existence. Work for that which you can't lose in him, and you will gain more than you can imagine.

In what ways can you utilize your time so that you receive a benefit that does not fade away?

_____

_____

_____

_____

_____

_____

_____

_____

_____

> *This is the work of God, that you believe on him*
> *whom God has sent.* (John 6:29)

Faith requires energy. It does not just happen without effort. You have to work at developing and maintaining faith. Working to establish a faith that can carry you through life is what God wants you to do. As you engage in the process of establishing strong faith, you will be doing the work of God. God desires that we do what we need in order to believe.

How are you working to develop strong faith that can carry you through life?

_____

_____

_____

_____

_____

_____

_____

_____

_____

> *Verily, verily, I say unto you, Moses gave you not that*
> *bread from heaven; but my Father gives you*
> *the true bread from heaven.* (John 6:32)

We give credit to those whom God uses as though God was not doing anything. We thereby misinterpret what God has done in times past. We misunderstand how to apply what has happened to our present time. We are misled by erroneous reflection on memorable instances of God's power and goodness. Jesus corrects our false notions by appropriately clarifying God's ability and activity and what it means. How often have we misinterpreted what God has done in ways that thwart what God intends?

What misinterpretations of what God has done in times past do you need Jesus to correct so you will clearly know the real meaning?

_____

_____

_____

_____

_____

_____

_____

_____

> *For the bread of God is he which comes down from*
> *heaven and gives life to the world.* (John 6:33)

Who feeds your faith so that you can grow to maturity? Who supplies your diet so that you are fed what is required to grow fully? Jesus Christ is the true great gift of God who comes to give life from heaven—bread that provides healthy nourishment for our faith development. Christ nourishes us by his example. He feeds us with his life that illustrates what true faith is really like.

In what ways is the life of Jesus providing nourishment for your faith to mature?

_____

_____

_____

_____

_____

_____

_____

_____

_____

_____

I am the bread of life. (John 6:35)

Feeding is necessary for nutrition. No sustained development and growth occurs without adequate nourishment, which comes from being fed. All sorts of diets are designed to promote proper growth, whether mental, physical, psychological, or spiritual. Jesus is the right provision we need to mature to our full faith stature. Get a steady diet of Jesus to mature fully.

What diet can you design with the provisions that Jesus makes available?

_____

_____

_____

_____

_____

_____

_____

_____

_____

He that comes to me shall never hunger. (John 6:35)

We spend our lives craving, desiring, longing, wanting, and yearning. Always searching for something, we want our hunger sated so that we are not continually driven by it. In a world where people are always hungry, Jesus offers the perpetual fulfillment we most need. In Jesus, you can continually realize the fulfillment of your desires.

In what ways can Jesus provide the fulfillment of your desires?

_____

_____

_____

_____

_____

_____

_____

_____

_____

_____

_____

_____

And he that believes on me shall never thirst. (John 6:35)

Not only is hungering a compelling feature of life, but so is its companion: thirst. They go together. You will not try to fulfill one without the other. One reminds us that we need nourishment. The other one reminds us that we need to be refilled in order to be refreshed. Jesus refills what has been depleted in our lives so that we can be refreshed for the rest of our lives. The Lord provides perpetual refills!

In what ways has Jesus replenished your life so that you could be renewed and refreshed?

_____

_____

_____

_____

_____

_____

_____

_____

_____

_____

_____

All that the Father gives to me shall come to me; and those
that come to me I will in no wise cast out. (John 6:37)

Coming to Christ is a choice. Those who choose Christ will be
received with open arms. No one will be turned away who accepts
God's offer of new life. Each one is given as an inheritance to Jesus
and as a possession that he will always keep.

How does the assurance of being secure in Christ equip you to
live more confidently?

_____

_____

_____

_____

_____

_____

_____

_____

_____

_____

For I came down from heaven, not to do my own will,
but the will of him that sent me. (John 6:38)

We often make choices with a hidden agenda or ulterior motive. Jesus declares that the intent of his coming into the world was for one purpose alone: to accomplish God's design of salvation as God's great agent. Jesus came of his own free will and accord, fulfilling the purpose of God to save humanity from the destruction we cause ourselves.

In what ways does the purpose of Jesus' life model for you how to live?

_____

_____

_____

_____

_____

_____

_____

_____

_____

_____

_____

_____

And this is the Father's will which has sent me, that of all which he has given me I should lose nothing, but should raise it up again at the last day. (John 6:39)

God desires Jesus to keep all who are in his care. That says it all. We have a promise from God. There is no better guarantee anywhere than that you are safe in the care of Christ.

How does the guarantee of your being kept safe in Christ encourage you to be more faithful?

_____

_____

_____

_____

_____

_____

_____

_____

_____

> *And this is the will of him that sent me, that every one which sees the Son, and believes on him, may have everlasting life: and I will raise him up at the last day.* (John 6:40)

There is so much that puts life at risk: accidents, natural disasters, and illness. God wills that we get beyond what jeopardizes life in order to be about the business of living fully. In Christ, God continues life beyond what threatens existence, giving us hope that there is so much more to life than what we know. Christ will have the last say about the inevitable outcome of human existence, that is, death.

How does your faith in Christ help you face that inevitable outcome?

_____

_____

_____

_____

_____

_____

_____

_____

_____

Does this offend you? (John 6:61)

Jesus shares some things that are difficult to comprehend. Difficulty is used as a reason for deserting or defecting, because that which is difficult generally requires what a person is not willing to give. Difficulty requires commitment to stay the course, discipline to avoid being detoured, and understanding to allow what is confusing.

How do you manage the difficulty associated with knowing and following Jesus?

_____

_____

_____

_____

_____

_____

_____

_____

_____

The Spirit is the one who gives life! Human strength can do nothing. The words that I have spoken to you are from that life-giving Spirit. (John 6:63, CEV)

A life-giving Spirit empowers existence. What you see is nothing more than a reflection of the spirit that causes life to be. There is truly a lot more to life than we can see. Jesus directs us to the Spirit behind existence, the source of life.

In what ways are you aware of the life-giving Spirit behind life?

_____

_____

_____

_____

_____

_____

_____

_____

_____

_____

_____

There are some of you that do not believe. (John 6:64)

The Lord knows who believes and who doesn't, whose love is counterfeit and whose devotion is real. Belief is not something you can fake. Either you believe or you do not. Your behavior as well as your speech will give you away.

In all honesty, how do you think the Lord would respond to you about your faith?

_____

_____

_____

_____

_____

_____

_____

_____

_____

_____

_____

Will you also go away? (John 6:67)

When the Lord says difficult things, some will desert and defect. It seems easier to run than to try to figure out what something baffling means. Jesus wants to know what you are going to do when you are faced with the difficulty associated with him and his teachings. How do you respond to the Lord's inquiry? Will you follow those who are leaving? Will you make a confession of faith that captures the trust you have in Christ based on your belief in him? What will you do?

How do you answer the Lord's query about your loyalty?

_____

_____

_____

_____

_____

_____

_____

_____

_____

_____

> *Can the blind lead the blind? Shall they not both*
> *fall into the ditch?* (Luke 6:39)

Here is a thought-provoking question worth considering. It raises an important concern about following anyone. How often do we blindly follow those who are equally blind? Be sure that whomever you are following can see where he or she is going. Otherwise you will be led to a less than desirable end.

In what ways are you prone to follow those who, due to lack of vision, will lead you astray?

_____

_____

_____

_____

_____

_____

_____

_____

_____

_____

> *I say unto you, I have not found so great faith,*
> *no, not in Israel.* (Luke 7:9)

Jesus marvels at few things. Great faith is one of them. Consider honestly for a moment your faith quotient. Do you have the kind of faith that would warrant Jesus using you as an example for others to emulate? How would Jesus evaluate your faith?

What is it about your faith that would cause Jesus to marvel, using you as an example for others to follow?

_____

_____

_____

_____

_____

_____

_____

_____

_____

_____

_____

> *Go your way, and tell John what things you have seen*
> *and heard; how that the blind see, the lame walk,*
> *the lepers are cleansed, the deaf hear, the dead are raised,*
> *to the poor the gospel is preached.* (Luke 7:22)

Jesus responds to an inquiry about his identity by informing the questioner about what he has done. Jesus offers his actions as proof of his credibility. Whenever you doubt who Jesus is, consider what he has done. His works speak for themselves.

What has Jesus done that settles your doubts about him?

_____

_____

_____

_____

_____

_____

_____

_____

_____

_____

And blessed is anyone who shall not be offended in me.
(Luke 7:23)

How can you expect to benefit from what you consider an insult?
Your belief arising from the results you see causes you to trust in
Jesus unequivocally. Trust brings a beneficial outcome, the blessing
that comes with the acceptance of Jesus.

In what ways has accepting Jesus blessed your life?

_____

_____

_____

_____

_____

_____

_____

_____

_____

_____

_____

_____

> *Who is this man in the wilderness that you went out*
> *to see? Did you find him weak as a reed, moved*
> *by every breath of wind?* (Luke 7:24, NLT)

Reflecting on the ministry of John the Baptist, Jesus ignites in the imagination characteristics of faithful discipleship. John was firm and not fickle as a reed shaking in the wind, blown by every gust of air making useless noise, going nowhere. No, John was directed and deliberate, consistent and courageous, focused and faithful. He was as clear about his responsibility as he was determined by his conviction.

How do you think Jesus would refer to the characteristic nature of *your* discipleship?

_____

_____

_____

_____

_____

_____

_____

_____

_____

_____

*Or were you expecting to see a man dressed in
expensive clothes? No, people who wear
beautiful clothes and live in luxury are found
in palaces, not in the wilderness.* (Luke 7:25, NLT)

As Jesus continues to describe John, he alludes to the quality of sacrifice. John was not clothed in soft garments and he did not live
mildly. He lived convincingly and powerfully. His witness was
more attractive than his appearance; his message drew people
more than any personal magnetism.

What qualities might Jesus see in you that would warrant his
citing you as an example for others?

But what went you out to see? A prophet? Yea, I say unto you, and much more than a prophet. (Luke 7:26)

Jesus commends John's life for being more than what his society deemed it was. He is greater than what is said about him. While his culture described him by what he did, Jesus says *who* he is. Don't let anyone limit all that you are by describing your life only by what they see. There is a lot more to you than what is said about you. You are much more than people can realize.

In what ways are you much more than what people see or say?

_____

_____

_____

_____

_____

_____

_____

_____

_____

_____

> *This is he, of whom it is written, Behold, I send*
> *my messenger before your face, which shall*
> *prepare the way before you.* (Luke 7:27)

John prepares the way for what is to happen. The quality of his life is not diminished; the role of his existence is not damaged. In fact, he becomes a bridge that links what was to what will be. In a sense, like John, we too have to prepare the way, becoming a bridge that connects yesterday with today as we point others to the way in Christ.

How are you a bridge to direct people from where they are to where they need to be?

_____

_____

_____

_____

_____

_____

_____

_____

_____

For I say unto you, among those that are born of women
there is not a greater prophet than John the Baptist:
but he that is least in the kingdom of God is
greater than he. (Luke 7:28)

Jesus heightens our understanding of what it means to be great with a comparison worth considering. Fulfilling your role in life makes you great. However, belief in what God does through the power of the Spirit in Christ makes you greater than great. So why settle for just great when you can be greater?

How does the assurance of a Spirit-empowered life heighten its value to you and others?

_____

_____

_____

_____

_____

_____

_____

_____

_____

> *How shall I describe this generation? With what*
> *will I compare them?* (Luke 7:31, NLT)

Some situations give us pause. One of them is unreasonably choosing to doubt no matter what the cost. We can be deliberately difficult because we want to keep distant. We manufacture the contradictory rationale to support that we are doing what we believe is real. The thing needed in this case is to describe what is taking place.

In what ways do you provoke the Lord to describe your behavior?

They are like a group of children playing a game in the public square. They complain to their friends, "We played wedding songs, and you weren't happy, so we played funeral songs, but you weren't sad." (John 7:32, NLT)

Games people play cheat them out of the very thing they want most in life. Like children, we play games where we are never satisfied. Whatever it is, it is not enough. Then we end up always being irritable and tough. What a sad commentary when what we want is so close at hand and yet we choose to cling to our dissatisfaction. We end up being a constant complainer.

How have you become a chronic complainer because of the games you are playing with yourself?

_____

_____

_____

_____

_____

_____

_____

_____

For John the Baptist came neither eating bread nor drinking wine; and you say, he had a devil. (Luke 7:33)

John was a recluse. He was isolated and remote. Some claimed he was possessed. Evidently, whatever the Lord does and however the Lord uses a person, someone will find fault with it. If you cannot be accepted for who you are, you will certainly not be accepted for being anyone else. Be true to yourself. People will think what they want anyway.

How have you permitted what others have said to determine how you understand yourself?

_____

_____

_____

_____

_____

_____

_____

_____

But because the Son of Man goes around eating and drinking, you say, "Jesus eats and drinks too much! He is even a friend of tax collectors and sinners." (Luke 7:34, CEV)

Jesus eats and drinks and associates with people. Some say he eats and drinks too much and keeps the wrong company. You know people are not honest when they complain about everything: this way is not right; that way is not right. Whatever it is, they find fault. Learn how to be confident in yourself, making allowance for those who have problems with you.

What do you need to do to be more confident in who you are?

_____

_____

_____

_____

_____

_____

_____

_____

_____

_____

Wisdom is justified of all her children. (Luke 7:35)

Wisdom produces its own children. There are those who recognize wisdom's voice and obey wisdom's teaching and follow wisdom's lead. They are all the evidence wisdom needs. You will know the tree by the fruit it bears.

How do you show yourself to be a child of wisdom?

_____

_____

_____

_____

_____

_____

_____

_____

_____

_____

_____

Simon, I have somewhat to say unto you. (Luke 7:40)

Imagine becoming irritated with the way someone expresses appreciation to Jesus for what he has done for him or her. Simon the Pharisee took offense and disapproved of Jesus' permitting what he considered to be an inordinate and inappropriate display of affection by a woman with a less than desirable reputation. Jesus has something to say to those who take offense at what people do to express their love for him as well as something to say to those who disapprove of what he permits.

What does the expression of lavish gratitude stir up in you: criticism, concern, or commendation?

_____

_____

_____

_____

_____

_____

_____

_____

_____

_____

> *There was a certain creditor which had two debtors:*
> *the one owed five hundred pence, and the other fifty.*
> *And when they had nothing to pay, he frankly*
> *forgave them both. Tell me therefore, which*
> *of them will love him most?* (Luke 7:41-42)

An analogy helps us to see ourselves as well as provide insights that we would probably ignore. The way gratitude finds expression is directly linked to the degree of our appreciation for what has been done. Where the perception is that little has been done, little gratitude is expressed. Where the perception is that much has been done, much gratitude is expressed.

What does your gratitude gauge tell you about the scope of what the Lord has done in your life?

You have rightly judged. (Luke 7:43)

We can rightly discern the lesson the Lord teaches when we are truthful with ourselves and personal bias is exposed. A right assessment involves being honest about what we want for ourselves that we would deny others. In some sense, our undeserved entitlement causes us to see someone else's privilege as being unjustified.

In what ways has your bias been exposed by the Lord when you have been honest in your assessment?

_____

_____

_____

_____

_____

_____

_____

_____

_____

_____

See this woman? I entered your house, you gave me no water for my feet: but she has washed my feet with her tears, and wiped them with the hairs of her head. (Luke 7:44)

Deep gratitude expresses itself with great courtesy that embarrasses others, because its lavishness exposes their negligence. Consumed with a sense of entitlement, we fail to offer even the most ordinary courtesies. In our attempts to justify our behavior, we demean someone else's. We are made aware by the way others' gratitude finds expression that maybe ours is greatly lacking.

How do you express gratitude? Do you neglect common courtesies?

_____

_____

_____

_____

_____

_____

_____

_____

_____

> *You gave me no kiss: but this woman, since the time I*
> *came in, has not ceased to kiss my feet.* (Luke 7:45)

The kiss, a gesture of hearty and affectionate welcome, says, "I am glad that you are in my life. I embrace you with open arms. I accept you tenderly. I put myself at your disposal graciously."

How does your affection for the Lord find expression?

My head with oil you did not anoint: but this woman has anointed my feet with ointment. (Luke 7:46)

Jesus commends unbridled gratitude even though he does not command it. Might it be a good idea to be lavish every once in a while in demonstrating our appreciation to the Lord? Imagine the Lord commending you for doing what you were not commanded to do. Your only compulsion was that your heart compelled you.

In what ways does you heart compel you to thank the Lord?

_____

_____

_____

_____

_____

_____

_____

_____

_____

_____

*Wherefore I say unto you, Her sins, which are many,
are forgiven; for she loved much: but to whom little
is forgiven, the same loves little.* (Luke 7:47)

It is good to know that the Lord defends the faithful, sincere, and loving response that meets with criticism. You do not always have to defend yourself. It would be useless anyway. The Lord has a way of defending us better than we can defend ourselves. There is nothing better than the sanction that comes from the Lord that you have provided an excellent example worth commending.

Can you think of a time when the Lord defended you when others were offended by what you did?

_____

_____

_____

_____

_____

_____

_____

_____

_____

AUGUST 22 🌿

Your sins are forgiven. (Luke 7:48)

The Lord frees us from what causes us to be continually stuck. We are victims of the intruding past. Yesterday tugs us away from today's opportunity and from initiating tomorrow's possibility. The Lord tells us that we are forgiven. We are free from the cramping confines of a pattern of behavior that would reinforce that from which we seek to escape. That is what it means to be forgiven: free from the specter of yesterday, so that you can embrace your today, looking forward to your bright tomorrow.

Can you think of areas in your life where freedom from the negative consequences of yesterday could help you get to the positive opportunities of tomorrow?

_____

_____

_____

_____

_____

_____

_____

_____

Your faith has saved you; go in peace. (Luke 7:50)

Faith provides what we need to get from where we are to where we want to be, beyond the boundary of a life that is lived in captivity. Faith frees us from yesterday's grasp so that we are open to receive tomorrow's hope. Faith carries us with unflagging desire for what God has in store and propels us to attain the prize of the high calling in Christ.

How has your faith made a difference in your life?

_____

_____

_____

_____

_____

_____

_____

_____

_____

_____

*A sower went out to sow his seed: and as he sowed,
some fell by the way side; and it was trodden down,
and the fowls of the air devoured it.* (Luke 8:5)

God's Word is the seed. Our hearts are the soil. When the Word goes
unnoticed, something contrary consumes it. It is eaten by whatever
comes along. Only when the Word is purposefully received as a seed
planted in the heart is fruit borne to the glory of God.

How can you prevent whatever comes along from consuming
the Word intended for you?

_____

_____

_____

_____

_____

_____

_____

_____

_____

_____

_____

And some fell upon a rock; and as soon as it was sprung up,
it withered away, because it lacked moisture. (Luke 8:6)

When the Word is received lightly, it cannot take root in order to grow. What results withers away because the environment cannot sustain the growth. The Word must be taken seriously in order for commitment and devotion to develop properly. Otherwise, dedication will decrease and fidelity will fade.

How can you prevent your dedication from decreasing and your fidelity from fading?

_____

_____

_____

_____

_____

_____

_____

_____

_____

_____

And some fell among thorns; and the thorns sprang
up with it and choked it. (Luke 8:7)

When the Word is received in a cluttered environment, opposing
interests vie for attention. Where the cares of life entangle the Word
of God, our desire to embrace it is suffocated. Our circumstances
smother us and strangle the life of the Word. We become stifled to
the point where it is difficult to believe.

What can you do to keep God's Word from being strangled within you?

_____

_____

_____

_____

_____

_____

_____

_____

_____

_____

> *And others fell on good ground, and sprang up,*
> *and bore fruit a hundredfold.* (Luke 8:8)

When the Word is genuinely received, the results are astonishing. A bountiful yield beyond imagining is produced. Permit the Word to find root in your life and define how you understand your circumstance instead of permitting your circumstance to define how you understand the Word. See what a difference that makes in the way your faith finds expression.

What helps you to be the good ground where God's Word is sown and bears fruit?

_____

_____

_____

_____

_____

_____

_____

_____

_____

Let anyone with ears to hear listen. (Luke 8:8)

It would be shameful to hear something that is profitable and miss the benefit because you did not pay attention. How often do we hear and not listen? How often do we misunderstand what is clear because we refuse to hear? It is as though we have an automatic eject system that filters out what we do not want to accept.

In what way(s) have you refused to hear what you knew you needed to hear?

_____

_____

_____

_____

_____

_____

_____

_____

_____

_____

> *For nothing is secret, that shall not be made manifest;*
> *neither anything hid, that shall not be known*
> *and come abroad.* (Luke 8:17)

Seeds bear fruit. The crop we see is the product of what we have sown, for we reap what we sow. What a prospect to consider when you do not like your life! It is exactly what you have made it. It has become precisely what you have grown it to be.

What are you making of your life with the seeds that you sow? What is the crop that you will eventually grow?

_____

_____

_____

_____

_____

_____

_____

_____

_____

_____

*Take heed therefore how you hear: for whosoever has,
to him shall be given; and whosoever has not, from him
shall be taken even that which he seems to have.* (Luke 8:18)

We are responsible for how we hear and how we process what is heard. The accuracy of our hearing and the truth of our understanding belong solely to us. When you utilize appropriately what has already been given, more will be made available. When you misuse what has been provided, you erode the possibility of its effectiveness, thereby reducing the probability of keeping it.

How can you be more responsible for hearing the truth of the Word of God so that you benefit rather than lose what it imparts?

_____

_____

_____

_____

_____

_____

_____

_____

_____

Where is your faith? (Luke 8:25)

In the midst of sudden, unexpected exposure to life-threatening danger, we are frightened. Our fear eclipses our faith. We sense our helplessness and wonder if the Lord cares. We cry out in our distress. The Lord makes us aware that we are not abandoned in our adversity and that we are safe in the Lord's care. Then the Lord wants to know what happened to our faith. Where did it go? Why do you let it leave?

What happens to your faith when you are threatened by sudden, unexpected, life-threatening danger?

_____

_____

_____

_____

_____

_____

_____

_____

_____

_____

What is your name? (Luke 8:30)

Our name is what we use to identify who we are. Our name is also a way that others refer to us. The perception we have of ourselves can be discerned by the way we introduce ourselves to others, by how we use our name. Sometimes we are unable to manage our reality because we are torn by conflict. Internal wrestling and external threats keep us from being in control. Reveal your true identity by telling the Lord who you really are: anxious, bewildered, disgusted, frustrated, helpless, indifferent, preoccupied.

What do you think will happen if you tell the Lord your real name?

_____

_____

_____

_____

_____

_____

_____

_____

_____

_____

*Return to your own house, and show the great things
God has done for you.* (Luke 8:39)

People who are the recipients of the Lord's mercy are obligated to
share what God has done for them with those with whom they
have a history. It has been said that charity begins at home.
Testifying and witnessing about the goodness of the Lord is a good
place to start. Who knows, this may be what those close to you
need to see so they may believe in the power of what God can do.

To whom do you need to give a testimony of the goodness of
God in your life?

_____

_____

_____

_____

_____

_____

_____

_____

_____

_____

Who touched me? (Luke 8:45)

We come to the Lord concealing our need because we are embarrassed about what is wrong with us. So we attempt to sneak in to get the relief we desire without anyone knowing, including the Lord. We blend with others, seeking the security of safety in numbers. When the opportunity presents itself, we seize the moment with great expectation. Before we can ease away, the Lord recognizes the touch of faith that has fulfilled its desire and bids the recipient to acknowledge what has taken place.

How do you fail to acknowledge what you have received in faith from the Lord?

_____

_____

_____

_____

_____

_____

_____

_____

_____

> *Somebody touched me, for I felt the power going*
> *out of me.* (Luke 8:46)

There are those who try to explain away or dismiss as frivolous the Lord's query. However, the Lord is clear about the difference in a casual touch, a brushing up against, and a touch of faith seeking help, an intense reaching out. The Lord knows the kind of touch that reaches out from pain hoping for some relief. While it is the delight of the Lord to address our maladies, nevertheless we have a responsibility to acknowledge what we have received.

What have you attempted to get from the Lord without acknowledging it?

> *You are now well because of your faith.*
> *May God give you peace!* (Luke 8:48, CEV)

Some say, "If you have the faith, the Lord has the power." Faith faces facts by reaching beyond what is anticipated. Faith adjusts our attitudes, controls our choices, and reinforces our resolve. Faith pushes us where we would not otherwise go. Faith carries us when we can't carry ourselves. Faith makes the difference in our lives. Faith can make the difference in your life.

How has your faith made a difference in your life?

_____

_____

_____

_____

_____

_____

_____

_____

_____

_____

> *Fear not: believe only, and she shall be made whole.*
> (Luke 8:50)

Just when we think we are on the right track, some interruption happens that throws us off and seems like a setback. Though it may be difficult, be encouraged even when setbacks take place. You will be surprised at the outcome if you have faith. A satisfactory outcome is possible even in the worst situation, if you believe. All things are possible if only you believe.

What would it take for you to believe through and beyond your trouble?

_____

_____

_____

_____

_____

_____

_____

_____

_____

Weep not; she is not dead, but asleep. (Luke 8:52)

Jesus shares words of comfort amid the ridicule and scorn of those who lack faith. We presume that we know better than the Lord about the reality of our situation. Therefore, it is difficult for us to accept in faith what Jesus offers as a possibility. Doubters offer their perspectives on the situation. Whose words will you hear in your time of distress? Whose voice will you permit to speak to your anguish?

In your distress, what does it take for you to accept the comfort that God provides in Christ?

Whom say the people that I am? (Luke 9:18)

What are people saying about Christ and who he is? Too often, Jesus reminds people of someone else—a prophet, a wise teacher, a miracle worker—which means that they are denying his unique identity. In denying the fullness of the Lord's true being, we cheat ourselves out of the full gift the Lord offers. We miss the opportunity to receive the life that the Lord gives.

How have you denied the Lord's true being by imposing an image that depicts what you miss or want? Do personal opinions of those who have something to say about Jesus influence your perception of Christ?

_____

_____

_____

_____

_____

_____

_____

_____

_____

Whom say you that I am? (Luke 9:20)

The personal opinions of the crowd can influence our understanding of Jesus. We need to make a distinction between personal opinions and passionate conviction. Faith is born of passionate conviction based on experience, not selfish opinions based on personal judgment. Jesus asks us about our passionate conviction concerning him. Who is he and what is he to you?

What is your passionate conviction about Jesus?

_____

_____

_____

_____

_____

_____

_____

_____

_____

_____

> *If any want to become my followers, let them deny*
> *themselves and take up their cross daily*
> *and follow me.* (Luke 9:23, NRSV)

Following Christ requires willingness to surrender selfish ambition for a loftier goal. We can be so self-absorbed that a sense of entitlement controls our thoughts and desires, and determines our choices. We can be so full of ourselves that we want everything to revolve around us as though we are the center of life. It takes a conscientious effort to say no to self-indulgence and yes to self-discipline. Those who would follow Jesus must be willing to discipline themselves so as to build strength to face life's adversities daily with courage.

In what ways do your selfish ambitions keep you from being self-disciplined as a believer?

_____

_____

_____

_____

_____

_____

_____

_____

_____

For those who want to save their life will lose it, and those who lose their life for my sake will save it. (Luke 9:24, NRSV)

Imagine losing to gain and gaining to lose. It sounds contradictory. However, Christ assures us that our benefits increase in him and our losses diminish. Without him, our losses multiply and our benefits decrease. Now this is something worth considering: we can become so consumed with preserving what we have that we miss new opportunities.

What do you gain in Christ that you would lose without him?

_____

_____

_____

_____

_____

_____

_____

_____

_____

_____

> *What will you gain, if you own the whole world but*
> *destroy yourself and waste your life?* (Luke 9:25, CEV)

Some things cost too much. They can be had at too great a price. Why sell yourself for anything? You are too precious and priceless to be sold at any cost. It is foolish to pay for what you cannot keep with what you do not want to lose.

   In what ways are you prone to lose yourself in order to get what you cannot keep?

_____

_____

_____

_____

_____

_____

_____

_____

_____

If you are ashamed of me and my message, the Son of Man
will be ashamed of you when he comes in his glory and in the
glory of his Father and the holy angels. (Luke 9:26, CEV)

Maybe one of the most difficult things for us to admit is that we are
prone to being ashamed of the Lord. Making excuses for our lack
of commitment is one way that we demonstrate that we are
ashamed of Christ and his message. We apologize for our beliefs so
as not to offend others. We make excuses for our faith. Our loyalty
is slack. When we are afraid to own what Christ says and teaches,
then Christ will disown us.

Have you made excuses for your lack of allegiance?

_____

_____

_____

_____

_____

_____

_____

_____

_____

_____

Forbid him not: for he that is not against us is for us.
(Luke 9:50)

We can be quite narrow-minded and bigoted in practicing our faith. We use our faith to control others rather than to confirm them and assist them in building their capacity to make life better. We use our faith to exclude others while we exalt ourselves. Jesus reminds us that we do not have a monopoly on the way faith is expressed in the world. Some make faith a reality by not opposing it.

How has your faith been limited in the way it finds expression in regard to embracing others?

_____

_____

_____

_____

_____

_____

_____

_____

> *You know not what manner of spirit you are of.*
> *For the Son of man is not come to destroy people's*
> *lives, but to save them.* (Luke 9:55-56)

What appears to be righteous zeal turns out to be nothing more than retaliation for being personally offended. We cloak our real intent under the guise of being driven by our faith. We mask our true motives behind our love and devotion to some larger purpose. It is frightening to think that we suggest doing something that is sinister in the name of what is sacred. How often has faithful zeal cloaked pride and personal revenge? Jesus is displeased and rebukes those persons motivated by passion who would harm those who reject Christ.

How have you used your faith to retaliate when you have been offended?

SEPTEMBER 16 ❧

> *No one, having put his hand to the plough, and looking*
> *back, is fit for the kingdom of God.* (Luke 9:62)

Some concerns can always get in the way of the commitment we
claim we are willing to make to the Lord. We may be unwilling to
enter new territory with the Lord or we deem other interests more
important; maybe other attachments tug at our hearts and require
immediate attention. When you resolve to follow the Lord, do not
be distracted by the unknowns or what you are leaving behind. If
you revisit what has been settled, you run the risk of being unfit to
proceed with your decision to go on with the Lord.

How have you permitted your expectations, other interests, or
what you are leaving behind to keep you from being totally
committed to the Lord?

_____

_____

_____

_____

_____

_____

_____

_____

_____

> *The harvest is great, but the laborers are few: pray
> you therefore the Lord of the harvest, that he would
> send forth laborers into his harvest.* (Luke 10:2)

There are more opportunities than you realize to heighten people's awareness about the reality of the Lord's presence in their lives. The Lord needs people who are willing to gather those who are ready. Can the Lord depend on you to harvest those who are waiting?

In what ways can Christ count on you to be someone who will harvest a crop for the Lord?

_____

_____

_____

_____

_____

_____

_____

_____

_____

_____

_____

> *He that is not with me is against me: and he that*
> *gathers not with me scatters.* (Luke 11:23)

It is not difficult to determine whether you are working with Christ or not. We make choices about our faith. We decide what we believe. Sometimes life is an either-or proposition. You are either with the Lord or against the Lord. There is no middle ground. Are you with the Lord? Can the Lord count on you?

How do you demonstrate that you are unequivocally with the Lord?

Blessed are they who hear the word of God and keep it.
(Luke 11:28)

It is a tragedy to receive what you need to know but fail to act on it. We hear what will make a difference but fail to apply it appropriately to our lives. We grab for what keeps us from having to change as we interpret what we are told according to an understanding that suits us. The Lord reminds us that we will be blessed when we translate what we hear into activity that changes our behavior. Otherwise, you can be full of knowledge that serves no purpose other than discussion for its own sake.

How have you failed to practice what you have heard?

_____

_____

_____

_____

_____

_____

_____

_____

_____

_____

> *But how terrible it will be for you Pharisees! For you are careful to tithe even the tiniest part of your income, but you completely forget about justice and the love of God. You should tithe, yes, but you should not leave undone the more important things.*
>
> (Luke 11:42, NLT)

We pick and choose parts of our faith to practice, most often prioritizing incorrectly. In doing so, we fail to take into consideration that faithfulness is more than our own ideas of pious acts. We ignore the important matters of love and justice, presuming that we are exempt from what we neglect because of what we do. Fulfilling our duty in one way does not exempt us from fulfilling other duties as well.

How have you focused on what you are doing but perhaps neglected the other important matters of love and justice as you practice your faith?

How terrible it will be for you Pharisees! For how you love the seats of honor in the synagogues and the respectful greetings from everyone as you walk through the markets!
(Luke 11:43, NLT)

We miss the purpose of faith when we use it for personal recognition. We turn what is of supreme importance into an opportunity for our personal display of piety. We make ourselves the center of attention, demanding to be seen, acting as though we are the only ones who know what faith means. Jesus corrects us to make us aware that none of us is really worthy to boast, for we are all equally the recipients of God's loving care.

How has your desire or need for personal recognition gotten in the way of your faith being demonstrated with humility?

_____

_____

_____

_____

_____

_____

_____

_____

_____

_____

*You teachers are in for trouble! You load people
down with heavy burdens, but you won't lift a finger
to help them carry the loads.* (Luke 11:46, CEV)

Some people create unnecessary obstacles for those who are trying
to develop and mature in their faith. To demonstrate authority and
exert control, they burden others with traditions that negate liber-
ties God allows and enslave them with what God never
commanded. Jesus frees us from pretenses created by people in
authority so that we may know God's design for how to measure
the reality of faith. Faith is not measured by what is imposed on
you as much as by what is made available to you. Faith frees you
to live a life that honors God and fulfills your existence.

How has your faith freed you to live a life that honors God?

_____

_____

_____

_____

_____

_____

_____

_____

Yes, you are really in for trouble! You build monuments to honor the prophets your own people murdered long ago.
(Luke 11:47, CEV)

Pretense does not mix well with faith. Commemorating what one despises as though it were revered is the epitome of insincerity. Faith faces reality and all of its challenges with determination and resolve, while deception denies what is real. We all pretend at times, but we should never go to the extreme of venerating what we don't believe. That is a defeat of faith, not its victory.

How has your faith kept you from living with deceitful delusions that would cause you to pretend?

_____

_____

_____

_____

_____

_____

_____

_____

_____

_____

You teachers of the Law of Moses are really in trouble!
You carry the keys to the door of knowledge
about God. But you never go in, and keep
others from going in. (Luke 11:52, CEV)

How much more malicious and devious can people be than to deliberately mislead those who count on them for direction? Having available the knowledge you and others need and using it to impede, rather than increase, understanding is a travesty. Jesus reproves those who confuse people about the Lord's activity in their midst. Some block the way to understanding for those who look to them for insight. Beware that one who knows what God requires and yet will not do it and also makes it harder for you to obey God.

In what ways can you discern if you are being taught incorrectly?

_____

_____

_____

_____

_____

_____

_____

_____

_____

> *Five sparrows are sold for two pennies, but God
> doesn't forget a one of them. Even the hairs on your head are
> counted. So don't be afraid! You are worth much more than
> many sparrows.* (Luke 12:6-7, CEV)

Jesus encourages us to consider what it means that God cares for
us. God's care extends further than we can realize. God even
notices the details of life that escape our eyes. We are safe in the
care of the Lord. Therefore, we do not fear what life can bring, for
God cares for us through everything. In God's care we discover the
security we need as well as the affirmation that we are important.
We are not afraid because we have the care of God to combat what
causes us dread.

How has God's providential care kept you from feeling insignificant and from being afraid?

_____

_____

_____

_____

_____

_____

> *Don't be greedy! Owning a lot of things will not*
> *make your life safe.* (Luke 12:15, CEV)

Jesus gives us a word of caution about hitching our lives to what can't possibly provide what we most desire. We want safety and security. We tend to think that wealth and riches will insulate us against the fear of uncertainty. Wealth will not suffice to keep us; neither does greed make life any better. The reality is, either we will leave things, or they will all leave us.

In what ways have you defined your life by what you have rather than by who you are?

_____

_____

_____

_____

_____

_____

_____

_____

_____

> *Who then is that faithful and wise steward, whom*
> *his lord shall make ruler over his household, to give*
> *them their portion of meat in due season?* (Luke 12:42)

The Lord desires faithfulness. Unfortunately, we permit some things to get in the way that detour us from being loyal. Delayed expectations are one, because we waver in our fidelity when what we anticipate is delayed. Selfish inclinations are another, as we dismiss our lack of devotion by permitting selfish passion to take control. Popular opinions get in the way when we excuse our unreliability and allow what is popular to determine how we reach our goal. This question of the Lord continues to resound with its challenge: "Who then is that faithful person on whom the Lord can depend?"

How have you permitted delayed expectations, selfish inclinations, and popular opinions to detour you from being faithful?

_____

_____

_____

_____

_____

_____

_____

_____

> *Servants are fortunate if their master comes and*
> *finds them doing their job.* (Luke 12:43, CEV)

Imagine how satisfying it is for you to be found doing what you are supposed to do. Oh, what a relief it is to be found reliably fulfilling your task! Hardly any description can adequately picture this reality. An approximation might be an image of everyone in their place doing what is expected within the frame of God's overarching purpose. What a delightful sight! Can you be counted among those whom the Lord finds doing their job as believers?

In what ways are you doing what the Lord expects of you as a believer?

_____

_____

_____

_____

_____

_____

_____

_____

_____

_____

> *A servant who is faithful will surely be put in charge of everything that the master owns.* (Luke 12:44, CEV)

Fidelity is rewarded. If you can be trusted with little, you will be trusted with much. Life has a way of adding incrementally to every faithful effort of consistent reliability. You get what you prove you can handle with more added when you demonstrate you can be trusted. Are you are a faithful believer who handles well the responsibility you have been given?

In what ways do you demonstrate your fidelity to your responsibility as a believer?

_____

_____

_____

_____

_____

_____

_____

_____

_____

_____

_____

But suppose one of the servants thinks that the master won't return until late. Suppose that servant starts beating all the other servants and eats and drinks and gets drunk. If that happens, the master will come on a day and at a time when the servant least expects him. That servant will then be punished and thrown out with the servants who cannot be trusted. (Luke 12:45-46, CEV)

Infidelity testifies to the inadequate and inappropriate inclinations that are determining and directing your behavior. You are motivated by some proclivity that drives you more than by the appreciation and devotion that should claim your allegiance. You attempt to second-guess when you will have to give an account of the activity of your life only to realize that you can't calculate when that time will come. Caught by surprise, you are found unreliable. The reward for being unfaithful is to be numbered among those who are considered untrustworthy.

In what ways have you been caught by surprise to give an account of your unreliable activity?

The servant will be severely punished, for though he knew
his duty, he refused to do it. (Luke 12:47, NLT)

We know more about right and good than we are willing to do.
Irresponsible behavior will be rewarded for what it is: careless, defi-
ant, foolish, negligent, and reckless. Sometimes we don't care. Other
times we are willful. Moreover, there are times when we are irresponsible or we want to see what we can get away with. Regardless
of the cause of disobedience, a price is paid. We finally discover in
the end that disobedience, regardless of its motivation, is costly.

How do you catch yourself ignoring what you know to do?

_____

_____

_____

_____

_____

_____

_____

_____

_____

But people who are not aware that they are doing wrong will be punished only lightly. Much is required from those to whom much is given, and much more is required from those to whom much more is given. (Luke 12:48, NLT)

Ignorance is not an acceptable excuse for negligence. A price is still paid even when you did not know what you were doing. Consequences follow choices, whether made with good intent or not. We can expect to benefit, however, from the knowledge we have been given. The more knowledge we have, the more we benefit.

In what ways have you been chastised for what you did not know?

You are loosed from your infirmity. (Luke 13:12)

From what do you need to be set free? What exactly is your infirmity? We all have an impairment of some kind in our lives. We are all bent or crippled in some way, shape, or fashion. We are all in need of help to straighten our lives. We are unable to do it by ourselves. It was in a special place on a special day that the Lord saw, spoke to, and touched a person crippled by infirmity. As you go to your special place on your special day, the Lord will see you, speak to you, and touch you in order to free you from what cripples you so that you can straighten up your life.

How has the Lord freed you from a spirit of infirmity that crippled you and bent your life out of shape?

Jerusalem, Jerusalem! Your people have killed the prophets and have stoned the messengers who were sent to you. I have often wanted to gather your people, as a hen gathers her chicks under her wings. But you wouldn't let me. (Luke 13:34, CEV)

Jesus laments the rejection of God's love expressed in him as a missed opportunity and a lost privilege. Life is filled with many instances where we can experience the love of God in Christ. This love of God in Christ is confirmed in the grace we continually receive, the freedom we have been given, and the love we offer others. Have you missed opportunities and lost the privilege to embrace the love of God in Christ because you just refused to see it?

In what ways have you missed opportunities and lost privileges to experience the love of God in Christ?

_____

_____

_____

_____

_____

_____

_____

_____

> *There are some things that people cannot do, but*
> *God can do anything.* (Luke 18:27, CEV)

There are some things we cannot do for ourselves. We cannot save ourselves from the consequences of our choices or the destruction we cause when we selfishly take what we want, or from the hurt we inflict when we are insensitive to the needs of others. Jesus tells us that God can do for us what we cannot do for ourselves. God can do the impossible. God can use the consequences of our choices to our advantage, reverse the effects of our selfishness, and repair the damage of our mistakes.

How have you experienced God doing the impossible in your life?

What were you talking about as you walked along?
(Luke 24:17, CEV)

Have you ever been discouraged because things did not work out as you had hoped and expected and all you could do was talk about your disappointment with someone else? While comfort can be found in the companionship of those who share their hurt with each other, confusion is relieved only with insight. Let the Lord interrupt your conversation about what you are going through. He will explain in such a way that you will understand clearly. The Lord brings encouragement in our distress. In your anguish, talk with Jesus.

How have you been encouraged in your times of disappointment by the Lord's explanation that brought helpful insight?

_____

_____

_____

_____

_____

_____

_____

_____

Peace be unto you. (Luke 24:36)

The Lord provides consolation when we are fearful and greets us with peace, making it quite clear that we have all the evidence we need to believe. The testimony of others and our experience confirm what God has done. In both, the reality of the Lord's presence is revealed.

How have the testimony of others and your experience confirmed the presence of the Lord in your life?

> *Why are you so frightened? Why do you doubt?*
> (Luke 24:38)

Fear and doubt go hand-in-hand. Where there is one, there is the other. You fear because you doubt and you doubt because you fear. Our fear comes because we are challenged to face what happens in life. Our doubt comes because we struggle with ourselves to manage our life. The Lord prompts us to consider the connection between the two. In doing that we can better see how to manage what we are going through.

What do you need to do to learn how to control you fear and manage your doubt?

_____

_____

_____

_____

_____

_____

_____

_____

_____

If you are thirsty, come to me and drink! (John 7:37, CEV)

We are all thirsty for something. We all have cravings, desires, longings, and yearnings of all sorts. We want assurance in our adversity, belief for our bewilderment, confidence for our crisis, comfort in our calamity, deliverance from our distress, faith for our frustration, grace for our guilt, mercy for our mistakes, peace for our perplexity, solace for our suffering, and triumph for our trouble. The Lord invites us to the fulfillment that only the Lord can give. In Christ, your needs in all of the changing scenes of your life can be satisfied.

How has the Lord quenched your thirst, satisfying your desire with what you needed most when there was a drought in your life?

Have faith in me, and you will have life-giving water flowing from deep inside you, just as the Scriptures say. (John 7:38, CEV)

Imagine having a resource at your disposal within yourself like a reservoir that you can tap into anytime. Faith in Jesus provides a sufficiency that is continually accessible in all of life's circumstances. In Christ you have all you need to face whatever comes your way. Not only that, but you have enough for others to benefit from what flows from your life.

In what ways has your faith in Jesus been a continual benefit to you and to those around you?

> *He that is without sin among you, let him cast*
> *the first stone at her.* (John 8:7)

Whenever we seek to condemn someone, Jesus disarms us by having us consider our faults and failures. Remember when you point a finger at someone else, you have three pointing back at you. We can always find someone else to condemn so that we can commend ourselves. However, Jesus exposes us for who we really are, uncovering the motives that cause us to do what we do, making us aware that those motives are not nearly always pure.

How are you disarmed from condemning someone else when you consider your faults and failures?

_____

_____

_____

_____

_____

_____

_____

_____

> *I am the light of the world. If you follow me, you won't*
> *be stumbling through the darkness, because you will have*
> *the light that leads to life.* (John 8:12, NLT)

In this solemn assertion, Jesus speaks figuratively of himself as the light that dispels darkness and enhances life. Light penetrates, pierces, and probes the darkness to the extent that the darkness no longer exists. The illumination from the life of Christ has provided all of the insight we need to see clearly. Jesus is the light that increases our understanding of God, improves our relationships with one another, and ignites our honest assessment of ourselves.

How has the light from the life of Jesus provided understanding to you about God, your relationship with others, and your assessment of yourself?

_____

_____

_____

_____

_____

_____

_____

_____

_____

If the Son gives you freedom, you are free! (John 8:36, CEV)

We adjust our interpretation of reality to the extent that we deny what has happened. We kid ourselves about who we are and what we have done and the privilege we enjoy. Jesus awakens us to what we would deny, that we've been living in captivity of some kind. We are captive to what controls and drives us, to what molds and shapes us, to what reminds us that we are frail creatures of clay and dust. Jesus gives us true freedom. He frees us from whatever confines and threatens our lives. He frees us to live abundantly in his name. He frees us to be accessible and available to God.

How has Jesus freed you from bondage?

_____

_____

_____

_____

_____

_____

_____

_____

_____

Do you believe in the Son of God? (John 9:35)

Odd though it may seem, some people of faith are so blinded by what they believe that they will not see what valid experiences teach. The authority of personal experience is a remedy to prejudice that comes from being too proud to admit we have believed in a lie. We are challenged by the Lord through our experience to declare what we have come to believe is true. Your interpretation of your experience of the Lord is more real to you than to anyone else. When you consider what the Lord has done for you, would you permit anyone else, through his or her interpretation of your experience of God, to determine what you believe?

How have you been challenged to affirm your faith based on your experience of the Lord?

Verily, verily, I say unto you, I am the door of the sheep.
(John 10:7)

A door presumes a within and a without. In order to get from one place to the other, we must go through. Through whom have you come to get to the reality of God's presence in your life? Often we come through others whose witness we trust. Other times we come through our ability to reason for ourselves. Or we come through the tradition in which we have been taught. Jesus says, "Come through me, for I am the true portal that leads to what you seek."

In what ways is Jesus the door for you to enter into the family of God?

_____

_____

_____

_____

_____

_____

_____

_____

_____

*I am the door: by me if anyone enters, he shall be saved, and
shall go in and out, and find pasture.* (John 10:9)

We gain admission to certain blessings through Jesus. He is the
door to preservation from destruction, to freedom to come and go,
to fulfillment. The promised benefits of those who enter through
Christ are salvation, liberty, and satisfaction. What marvelous benefits they all are indeed!

How have the salvation, liberty, and fulfillment Jesus provides
benefited you?

_____

_____

_____

_____

_____

_____

_____

_____

_____

_____

> *I am the good shepherd. I know my sheep,*
> *and they know me.* (John 10:14, CEV)

This symbolic language captures a comforting thought. Three basic characteristics of Jesus as the good shepherd are that he is reliable, knowledgeable about us, and knowable by us. We can count on Jesus to care for us. We can rely on Jesus to know who we are. We can depend on Jesus to reveal to us who he is.

How has your faith been strengthened by the thought that Jesus is reliable, knowledgeable, and knowable?

Just as the Father knows me, I know the Father, and
I give up my life for the sheep. (John 10:15, CEV)

Jesus knows and is known by God, because their intimate relationship carries with it certain privileges. Some knowledge about God, such as God's sacrificial heart, can be had only through Jesus. With God's permission Jesus puts himself in harm's way to protect those who belong to God as well as to reflect the depth of the love of God.

In what ways does the sacrificial nature of God, as expressed in Christ, assure you of the protection and preservation you need to sustain your life?

_____

_____

_____

_____

_____

_____

_____

_____

_____

> *And other sheep I have, which are not of this fold: them*
> *also I must bring, and they shall hear my voice; and*
> *there shall be one fold, and one shepherd.* (John 10:16)

Here is another testimony that God does not support bigotry, prejudice, or narrow-mindedness. Jesus includes those we may be prone to exclude. We are not aware of all who belong to Christ. They will come when he calls and we will know they are his. We must of necessity concede that the Lord's authority exceeds anyone's right to determine who is in and who is out. We are all sheep anyway, which do not do the choosing but simply enjoy the privileges of being chosen.

In what ways do you need to concede to the authority of the Lord in choosing those who are part of the fold?

_____

_____

_____

_____

_____

_____

_____

_____

_____

No one takes my life from me. I give it up willingly! I have the power to give it up and the power to receive it back again, just as my Father commanded me to do. (John 10:18, CEV)

Here is a deliberate choice to sacrifice oneself for the sake of saving others. Jesus surrenders himself without coercion. He willingly gives his life to save those he loves. Choosing to give your life is the ultimate expression of love and care. Jesus' love is demonstrated in the sacrifice of his life for us. What does it mean to you that Jesus was willing to give his life?

How have you benefited from the gift of Jesus' life?

_____

_____

_____

_____

_____

_____

_____

_____

_____

_____

> *My sheep hear my voice, and I know them,*
> *and they follow me.* (John 10:27)

Relationship presupposes communication. Listening and hearing are two aspects of communicating. Both are active rather than passive and require a conscientious effort. Often we let someone else talk without listening, waiting to say what we want to say. Jesus says that those who belong to him hear what he says. You can't know who the Lord is and what the Lord means until you listen closely and process what the Lord says. Just as relationship presupposes communication, the need to hear means we do not yet know and when we know, we will listen even more.

How can you increase your capacity to better hear what the Lord says so that you can respond positively to what you hear?

And I give them eternal life; and they shall never perish, neither shall anyone pluck them out of my hand. (John 10:28)

What greater assurance can we have than to know that we are safe in the Lord's care? That is the guarantee that comes with being in relationship with the Lord as the Good Shepherd, the One who watches over us, cares for us, provides for us, and protects us from what threatens us. Nothing can separate us from the protective and preserving power of the Lord. We cannot be taken from that loving, living, and everlasting care. We are guaranteed this security. We are safe in the Lord's care.

What does it mean to you that you are safe in the Lord's care?

I am the resurrection and the life: he that believes in me, though he were dead, yet shall he live: And whosoever lives and believes in me shall never die. Do you believe this?
(John 11:25-26)

Ah, what hope these words engender, and what possibility they raise! Imagine, resurrection—to bring to life again. The sheer enormity of their meaning is so immense that it is better felt than told, better experienced than explained. Here is truth too deep and profound for human speech. Countless people have been raised from ruin to new life in Jesus and attest to being new creatures in him. Jesus gives us the promise of future life despite what threatens to end life. What do you think of this?

How has Jesus been the resurrection and the life for you?

_____

_____

_____

_____

_____

_____

_____

_____

_____

_____

_____

> *You don't really know what I am doing,*
> *but later you will understand.* (John 13:7, CEV)

Has something puzzling become clear to you in retrospect? Hindsight is 20/20. The Lord patiently acknowledges that we may not comprehend what he is doing in our lives right now, but later it will all become plain. The Lord provides the experience that will later help interpret what we can't seem to understand.

In what ways has understanding come to you about what the Lord was doing after the fact that you could not comprehend before the fact?

_____

_____

_____

_____

_____

_____

_____

_____

_____

Do you understand what I have done? (John 13:12, CEV)

We often fail to realize what the Lord is doing. Our impulsive response reflects our lack of understanding. The Lord wants us to answer whether or not we understand what is happening in our lives. More often than not we misunderstand what the Lord is doing because of our preconceived notions of what we want the Lord to do.

In what ways have you misunderstood what the Lord was doing in your life?

_____

_____

_____

_____

_____

_____

_____

_____

_____

_____

_____

> *I have set the example, and you should do for each other*
> *exactly what I have done for you.* (John 13:15, CEV)

Imitation is a common practice among people. Many of our habits are acquired from emulating others. Jesus reprograms our way of being in relationship by setting forth an example for us to follow. He challenges cultural norms and social standards by modeling an alternative way of behaving toward and with each other. Jesus challenges us to follow his example rather than continue with previously accepted patterns of behavior.

How are you challenged by the example of Jesus to change your behavior in relationship with other people?

_____

_____

_____

_____

_____

_____

_____

_____

_____

_____

> *But I am giving you a new command. You must love each other, just as I have loved you.* (John 13:34, CEV)

Jesus asks us to love one another as we have been loved by him. How has Jesus loved us? Jesus has loved us constantly, devotedly, practically, and sacrificially. The bond that knits believers together is their mutual love for the Lord expressed in their love for each other. Learning to live with those who we cannot live without requires that we love each other as God has loved us in Christ.

What do you have to do to love others constantly, devotedly, practically, and sacrificially, as Christ has loved you?

_____

_____

_____

_____

_____

_____

_____

_____

_____

_____

> *If you love each other, everyone will know that*
> *you are my disciples.* (John 13:35, CEV)

Jesus says that we will be known by the way we behave with each other. The badge of our identity as disciples is the way we love one another. Learning to love as Christ has loved us is the goal for which we strive. The way that people will know we are Christian is by our love. As you consider the way we express our faith, are you convinced that we reflect the love we have received?

In what ways can you demonstrate the love you have received by loving others?

_____

_____

_____

_____

_____

_____

_____

_____

_____

_____

> *Let not your heart be troubled: you believe in God,*
> *believe also in me.* (John 14:1)

Jesus offers us the assurance of faith amid life's awful agony, conflicting cares, and disquieting despair. When life closes in on you and you don't know what to do, your faith provides confidence to believe in God. Faith in God is equal to any emergency, and your belief is more than adequate for any confusion. When faced with the pain of betrayal, confusion, denial, and separation, put your trust in God.

How has your faith helped you get through difficulty in your life?

_____

_____

_____

_____

_____

_____

_____

_____

In my Father's house are many mansions: if it were not so, I would have told you. I go to prepare a place for you. (John 14:2)

Jesus gives us assurance for our anxiety when the inevitable outcome of life occurs. He tells us that we are not placeless. When we are separated from those we love, we still have a place. Not just any place but a *prepared* place. This is the assurance Jesus gives to settle our doubts and calm our fears when we are displaced. We are simply relocated to another place that has been prepared just for us. There is a future that we have yet to see beyond anything we can imagine.

How do the assurances Jesus gives help settle your doubts and calm your fears?

_____

_____

_____

_____

_____

_____

_____

_____

_____

> *And if I go and prepare a place for you,*
> *I will come again, and receive you unto myself;*
> *that where I am, there you may be also.* (John 14:3)

We have a consoling promise that we will be escorted to the place prepared for us when we exit this ephemeral reality and move to that "from whose shore no traveler returns." It is as if you have a personal guide assigned to come and take you where you are going. Since you don't know where it is or how to get there, you need to know that provision has already been made to get you there. You will be taken to the future by the very One who makes it a reality.

How does believing in Christ alleviate anxiety about the future beyond the reality we see?

_____

_____

_____

_____

_____

_____

_____

_____

> *I am the way, the truth, and the life: no one comes
> to the Father, but by me.* (John 14:6)

We all need a guide to help us get through life. Everyone follows
someone's advice. Jesus offers himself as the One who can lead us
to God. Jesus is the way to discover the reality of God's presence.
He is the truth about where God's presence can be discerned in the
world and the life that fulfills the purpose for which God has made
the world. If you really want to know God, look at Jesus. We can
measure the reality of those who have come to know God by how
closely they follow the example of Christ. In Christ you can see the
fullness of God expressed.

How is Jesus the way, the truth, and the life for you to discern
the presence of the Lord in your life and in the world?

_____

_____

_____

_____

_____

_____

_____

_____

_____

> *If you love me, you will do as I command.*
> (John 14:15, CEV)

Love and obedience are connected. You will do what those you love ask you to do because they asked you. You trust them because you know them. Love will not ask anything that is harmful to another but would only want what is best. Love finds its ultimate expression as an act of the will, even though emotion is associated with it. Love wills to do what expresses itself as true. Love determines how to be revealed in activity that is authentic and genuine. Love establishes the boundaries and limits by which it will operate.

In what ways does your love cause you to surrender in obedience to the Lord and to others with whom you have an intimate relationship?

_____

_____

_____

_____

_____

_____

_____

_____

And I will pray to the Father, and he shall give you another Comforter, that he may abide with you forever. (John 14:16)

The promise of a divine friend who will abide with us forever speaks to one of the deepest needs of humanity: not to be abandoned. You are not left alone, nor are you ever forsaken. The Comforter stands alongside you and works in and through you to strengthen you to face life despite difficulty. This One is faithful in admonition, gracious in encouragement, sympathetic and wise in counsel. Jesus promises this to us always.

How has the Lord's abiding presence strengthened you to face life and keep going despite any type of difficulty?

_____

_____

_____

_____

_____

_____

_____

_____

_____

> *I will not leave you comfortless: I will come to you.*
> (John 14:18)

The literal meaning of "comfortless" is "orphan." Orphans do not have protection or sponsorship. They are on their own. They fend for themselves. Jesus assures us that we will not be bereft of adequate security or support. We have the assurance that we are not the only ones fending for us, because the Lord comes and fends with us.

How has the abiding presence of Christ through the power of the Holy Spirit been a source of security and support for you?

_____

_____

_____

_____

_____

_____

_____

_____

*But the Comforter, which is the Holy Ghost, whom
the Father will send in my name, he shall teach
you all things, and bring all things to your
remembrance, whatsoever I have said unto you.*
(John 14:26)

The abiding presence of Christ—the Holy Spirit—who accompanies us through life is a source of security and support and also is a tutor. That abiding presence guides, guards, and teaches us as the Spirit of truth to understand our responsibility as believers. We are to pass on what we have received from the Lord. The abiding presence serves to remind us what the Lord said and meant in order to avoid any misinterpretation.

How have you been reminded of what the Lord said and meant by the abiding presence of the Holy Spirit?

_____

_____

_____

_____

_____

_____

_____

_____

I give you peace, the kind of peace that only I can give.
It isn't like the peace that this world can give.
So don't be worried or afraid. (John 14:27, CEV)

A gift derives value from the giver. What comes from Christ has the value-added peace that only Jesus can give. It fills us with sublime joy as it settles doubts and fears that abound in this world with a new creation of peace. This essential blessing would be greatly missed if you had to barely make it through life plagued with doubt.

How can you preserve the gift of peace that Jesus provides and keep your peace of mind even when tempted to be worried or afraid?

I am the true vine, and my Father is the gardener.
(John 15:1, CEV)

The vine is an emblem of Christ as the source of life as the gardener is representative of God's relationship to Jesus and to us. Christ, the vine, causes us to grow and make known the presence of God his Father. Life is a mutual, interlocking network of dependencies. Our connections feed us and fill us as we derive from them what we need to live and give back to them as we receive. There is give and take. Our associations are an indication of what we consider important and necessary. Jesus is the true vine to which we are connected as believers to achieve our ultimate possibility.

How does your connection to Jesus nourish your potential as a person?

_____

_____

_____

_____

_____

_____

_____

_____

He cuts away every branch of mine that doesn't produce fruit. But he trims clean every branch that does produce fruit, so that it will produce even more fruit. (John 15:2, CEV)

Pruning is necessary in order to promote growth. Some things need to be taken away in order for growth to occur. Sometimes we have to be purged so that we can become more productive. Our functioning may be faulty, because something is in the way. Pruning gets rid of what prevents us from being fruitful.

What does the Lord need to trim from you to increase your productivity?

_____

_____

_____

_____

_____

_____

_____

_____

Stay connected to me, and I will stay joined to you.
Just as the branch cannot produce fruit unless it is
stays joined to the vine, you cannot produce fruit
unless you stay joined to me. (John 15:4, CEV)

We have the privilege of sharing in the life of Christ. However, in order to share in that life we must take responsibility for being connected to Jesus. The privilege is the gift Jesus make available. The responsibility is the way we accept the gift of privilege to share the life of Christ.

What can you do to maintain your connection to Jesus so that you can share in the life of Christ?

_____

_____

_____

_____

_____

_____

_____

_____

_____

I am the vine, and you are the branches. If you stay joined to me, and I stay joined to you, then you will produce lots of fruit. But you cannot do anything without me. (John 15:5, CEV)

Remaining connected to Jesus is the key to being productive. We reproduce that to which we are attached. Being attached to Jesus equips us to produce a life that glorifies God and makes Christ real to others. We produce the fruit that was part of Jesus' life, the fruit of the Spirit: love, joy, peace, patience, kindness, generosity, faithfulness, gentleness, and meekness. We cannot produce this fruit unless we are attached to their source, to Jesus the Christ.

In what ways can you strengthen your attachment to the Lord so as to produce the fruit of the Spirit?

If you don't stay joined to me, you will be thrown away.
You will be like dry branches that are gathered
up and burned in a fire. (John 15:6, CEV)

The awful consequence of disconnecting from Christ is separation from the source of life. We lose our ability to fulfill our purpose. We lose our capacity for productivity. We lose the potential of our possibility. We lose all the way around. Separation causes fruitlessness, lives that are barren and ultimately useless. That contradicts the goal of existence to be fruitful and multiply, to be continually replenishing.

What can you do to prevent your life from becoming barren and worthless as a believer?

_____

_____

_____

_____

_____

_____

_____

_____

> *Stay joined to me and let my teachings become a part of you. Then you can pray for whatever you want, and your prayer will be answered.* (John 15:7, CEV)

The prerequisite to praying properly is prescribed here. Naming and claiming it is not mentioned. First, your connection to Jesus shapes your prayer life. Second, your prayers are governed by what Jesus taught. Then you can ask what you will and your prayer will be answered. That presupposes that you will not ask for anything for which Jesus would not ask, because it is Jesus' life and teachings that inform your praying as well as your living. Like Jesus, you will be asking for what you need to fulfill God's purpose in the world through you.

What do you need to fulfill God's purpose in the world through you?

When you become fruitful disciples of mine, my
Father will be honored. (John 15:8, CEV)

Jesus wants us to know that God is honored when we fulfill our
purpose as believers, bearing genuine fruit and in great quantity. To
live a life that honors God is the basic desire of a faithful believer.
After all, we come from God. We are made in God's image and
likeness. Something in us keeps us wanting to honor the divinity
that is in us. Producing fruit honors God.

In what ways does your life honor God?

_____

_____

_____

_____

_____

_____

_____

_____

_____

_____

I have loved you, just as my Father has loved me. So remain
faithful to my love for you. (John 15:9, CEV)

The love that Jesus has given to us is a reflection of the love that
Jesus received from God. They are one and the same. The way
Jesus is loved by God is the way Jesus loves us, and the way that
Jesus loves us is the way that God loves Jesus. The way we can be
faithful to the love Jesus has for us is to love as he has loved us. To
the extent that we accept the love of God in Christ, we too become
loving persons like Christ.

How can you demonstrate your faithfulness to the love you have
received from Christ?

_____

_____

_____

_____

_____

_____

_____

_____

_____

*When you obey me, you remain in my love, just as I obey my
Father and remain in his love.* (John 15:10, NLT)

We often act in ways that deny the love we have received, such as
by taking it for granted or abusing the privilege of being loved by
God. We disregard what accepting love means by ignoring limits
that are voluntarily imposed when love is received. We are negligent
in fulfilling love's obligations to be faithful.

We can show our appreciation of being loved by accepting the
restraints that love imposes. We can do what pleases the One who
loves us just as Jesus did what pleased God. As disciples, we are
expected to do what pleases Jesus.

In what ways have you been negligent in adhering to what Jesus
asks of you?

_____

_____

_____

_____

_____

_____

_____

_____

I have told you this so that you will be filled with my joy.
Yes, your joy will overflow! (John 15:11, NLT)

Love produces joy. Anyone who is loved or who loves is filled with unquestionable delight. Jesus wants us to experience the joy that comes with being loyal in our relationship with him as he did in his relationship with God. Joy that accompanies fidelity is unsurpassed by any other. Excitement of fulfillment and the thrill of victory because of faithfulness are unparalleled.

In what areas of life do you need to be more loyal in order to experience unequaled joy?

_____

_____

_____

_____

_____

_____

_____

_____

_____

*This is my commandment, that you love one another
as I have loved you.* (John 15:12)

Jesus admonishes us to follow his pattern as a precedent in our
behavior toward one another: "Love each other as I have loved
you." Jesus loved us sacrificially. He was willing to give his life so
that we all could learn how to live. The example Jesus provides
is one that challenges us to learn how to build our capacity to
love sacrificially.

Is there someone you can begin loving like Jesus loved you?

_____

_____

_____

_____

_____

_____

_____

_____

_____

_____

> *Greater love no one has than this, that he lay down his life for his friends.* (John 15:13)

It has been said that "if all that a person has he or she will give for his or her life, then the person who gives his or her life gives all that he or she has." Jesus gave all that he had for us. That is astounding. No wonder it evokes awe and reverence. We call it *amazing* grace, because we have not seen love on this order before.

In what ways have you experienced the amazing grace of God in Christ giving all he has and is for you?

_____

_____

_____

_____

_____

_____

_____

_____

_____

You are my friends, if you do whatsoever I command you.
(John 15:14)

Friendship is a two-way street, requiring commitment on the part of both parties involved. The Lord makes a commitment to us to be our friend. We in turn make a commitment to the Lord to respond in kind. Mutual reciprocity is the bond that holds the relationship together, making the association one of allegiance rather than one that abuses privileges. That is why it is called friendship; neither party uses the other selfishly. The relationship operates within certain parameters.

Have you accepted the Lord's friendship while neglecting to be a friend to the Lord?

> *Henceforth I call you not servants; for the servant does*
> *not know what his lord does: but I have called*
> *you friends; for all things that I have heard*
> *of my Father I have made known to you.*
> (John 15:15)

The true nature of friendship is intimacy. Sharing of a personal and confidential nature takes place. Friends don't play hide and seek or peek-a-boo. They share with each other plans that are important and significant to know. Jesus shares with us what God has told him so that we too can be privy to what he knows. We don't have to guess or wonder because we have now been told.

In what ways have you been told what you needed to know to make of your life something more?

_____

_____

_____

_____

_____

_____

_____

_____

> *You have not chosen me, but I have chosen you,*
> *and ordained you, that you should go and bring forth*
> *fruit, and that your fruit should remain: that whatsoever*
> *you shall ask of the Father in my name, he may give it to you.*
> (John 15:16)

Being chosen is a privilege. It suggests that we are sought out for who we are for special reasons. The Lord has chosen us through the power of the Spirit to let our life reveal what the grace of God can do. The benefit that accompanies such a privilege is that we have a source available to us to supply what we need to be productive continually. We can ask what we need with the assurance that we will receive it.

How does your life reveal to others what the grace of God in Christ can do?

_____

_____

_____

_____

_____

_____

_____

*Remember the word that I said unto you, the servant
is not greater than his lord. If they have persecuted me,
they will also persecute you; if they have kept
my saying, they will keep yours also.* (John 15:20)

Jesus prepares us to face the responsibility of being a faithful believer by reminding us that people will behave toward us like people behaved toward Jesus. Emulating the example of Jesus critiques the custom of our culture, the ritual of our religion, and the standards of our society. By calling established practices into question, you, like Jesus, will be mistreated, misunderstood, and ridiculed. As you fulfill your responsibility, prepare accordingly to face the challenge of hardship and remember the example of Jesus.

In what ways does the example of Jesus encourage you to be courageous as you challenge the custom of your culture, the ritual of your religion, and the standards of your society?

_____

_____

_____

_____

_____

_____

_____

I have told you these things so that you won't fall away.
(John 16:1, NLT)

To be forewarned is to be forearmed, so that we are not disillusioned by false expectations and terrified when trouble comes. Jesus prepares us to face the conflict as well as the challenge we will confront by telling us what to expect. We do not need to go along to get along or to withdraw. We can, like our Master, go forth into the battle unafraid, facing with courage and confidence what is ahead.

How does being forewarned prepare you to face challenges courageously and with confidence?

_____

_____

_____

_____

_____

_____

_____

_____

_____

Nevertheless I tell you the truth; it is expedient for you that I go away: for if I go not away, the Comforter will not come unto you; but if I depart, I will send him unto you. (John 16:7)

With separation and loss come gain and increase. We are given what we need to continue fulfilling our destiny. The Lord assures us of a constant and abiding presence in all of life's changing scenes that provides the insight and strength we need to make it. What a blessed assurance it is to know that we are not abandoned when separation occurs.

How have you been comforted and strengthened when you have experienced separation and loss?

_____

_____

_____

_____

_____

_____

_____

_____

_____

_____

*I have yet many things to say to you, but you
cannot bear them now.* (John 16:12)

The Lord does not overload us with what we cannot understand
but gives us just enough of what we need a little at a time. Learning
takes place in stages. No one learns everything all at once. We build
on what we know from our experiences each day. As we grow and
mature, then we will be in a better position to learn more of what
we are being told.

In what ways have you been able to build a little at a time on
the knowledge you have learned through your experience with
the Lord?

_____

_____

_____

_____

_____

_____

_____

_____

_____

*These things have I spoken to you, that in me you might
have peace. In the world you shall have tribulation: but
be of good cheer; I have overcome the world.* (John 16:33)

Our encouragement comes from the assurance Jesus provides. The precious legacy that Jesus gives to us is peace. We can confront our adversity with assurance, our crisis with courage, and our frustration with faith, all because Jesus has already overcome what we face. We can be of good cheer because we can see our way clear to follow the example of Jesus.

How do you have peace in, through, and by Jesus?

_____

_____

_____

_____

_____

_____

_____

_____

_____

READ JOHN 17 IN ITS ENTIRETY AS THE FOCUS OF the selections for the next twelve days (November 27–December 8). The prayer that Jesus prayed to the Father on behalf of his followers is recorded there and will be the basis of the thoughts that follow.

I told my followers what you told me, and they accepted it.
They know that I came from you, and they believe that
you are the one who sent me. (John 17:8, CEV)

Jesus acknowledges the purpose of his life in prayer. He was here to help us be aware of the presence of the Lord in our midst. As you begin to pray, maybe that is a good place to start. Begin by acknowledging how God has been present in your life.

How can you acknowledge prayerfully that the Lord has been present to you?

_____

_____

_____

_____

_____

_____

_____

_____

_____

Holy Father, I am no longer in the world. I am coming to you, but my followers are still in the world. So keep them safe by the power of the name that you have given me. (John 17:11, CEV)

God keeps us at Jesus' request. You could not ask for anything better than to be kept by God. Jesus wants us kept to fulfill our purpose in the world as he fulfilled his purpose. As we pray, we can ask God to be kept for Jesus' sake to fulfill our purpose of heightening people's awareness of where God is at work in the world.

In what ways have you been kept to heighten the awareness of what God is doing in the world?

Then they will be one with each other,
just as you and I are one. (John 17:11, CEV)

Divisiveness is a serious problem for believers. We are so fractured and fragmented. Our lack of cohesiveness does not present a true picture of the relationship that exists between God and Jesus. The Lord wants us kept so that we can truly reflect the harmonious way in which God operates through diversity. The Lord's prayer for us is that we get along in perfect harmony.

How can you begin to reflect the unity that exists with God as you fulfill your purpose to witness to his presence in the world?

_____

_____

_____

_____

_____

_____

_____

_____

*I am on my way to you. But I say these things while I
am still in the world, so that my followers will have the
same complete joy that I do.* (John 17:13, CEV)

We are reminded that joy is not predicated on circumstances.
Though the situation seems bleak, Jesus has complete joy. His joy
comes from a fulfilled life. This is the joy that Jesus passes on to us.
Fulfill the purpose for your existence so that you too can have the
joy that Jesus prays for you to have in him.

What would it take for you to experience the joy of which Jesus
speaks and wants for you?

Father, I don't ask you to take my followers out of the world, but keep them safe from the evil one. (John 17:15, CEV)

Jesus prays that believers will be kept from participating in the evil in the world. No one is exempt from exposure to the destruction that evil causes. The Lord's concern is not that we escape reality but that we develop a discerning faith that can detect and overcome evil.

How does your faith equip you to discern and overcome the evil in the world?

_____

_____

_____

_____

_____

_____

_____

_____

_____

_____

> *Your word is the truth. So let this truth make*
> *them completely yours.* (John 17:17, CEV)

In addition to bringing joy, the truth of God also brings power to live a God-honoring life. A life that honors God is a life that is consecrated and hallowed for sacred purposes and devoted to godly causes. The truth of the Word of God sets persons apart for this kind of life. They are enlightened, encouraged, equipped, and enabled to honor God. They are confirmed by the power of the Spirit as their faith sustains and strengthens them to transform the world.

In what ways does the truth of God in Scripture consecrate your life to honor God?

_____

_____

_____

_____

_____

_____

_____

_____

_____

I am sending them into the world, just as you sent me.
(John 17:18, CEV)

Being sent into the world by Jesus suggests that we are here with an exclusive and specific responsibility. We did not just happen to show up. We were specially prepared to be where we are and doing what we are doing. We are delegates who have a badge of identity that distinguishes us as confirmed and certified representatives. We have been sent and did not simply go.

How would you describe what you have been sent by Christ to do in the world?

_____

_____

_____

_____

_____

_____

_____

_____

_____

I am not praying just for these followers. I am also praying for everyone else who will have faith because of what my followers will say about me. I want all of them to be one with each other, just as I am one with you and you are one with me. I also want them to be one with us. Then the people of this world will believe that you sent me. (John 17:20-21, CEV)

Jesus prays for all believers in every generation throughout the ages. Jesus included everyone, from those first disciples to those yet to be persuaded by the faith of those who believe in Christ. Jesus prayed for our preservation, our sanctity, and our unity. He prays that we will be one in the Spirit and one in the Lord with each other. This is the desire of the Lord who established the Church. What better clue could we have about the way our faith witnesses to who Jesus is than what Jesus says here?

How is your faith strengthened by Jesus' prayer for you as it provides a picture of the Church?

I have honored my followers in the same way that you honored me, in order that they may be one with each other, just as we are one. I am one with them, and you are one with me, so that they may become completely one. Then this world's people will know that you sent me. They will know that you love my followers as much as you love me. (John 17:22-23, CEV)

The theme of unity is so important that Jesus repeats it. It cannot be overemphasized. So central and key is it for believers' witness in the world that Jesus mentions it again. The love that God has for Jesus is the same love that we experience in Christ as a bond that unites us in mutual concern and endeavor. The only way to identify Jesus' followers is by the way they love each other and by the way they live together in the world.

In what ways can you fulfill Jesus' desire for unity among believers?

_____

_____

_____

_____

_____

_____

_____

Father, I want everyone you have given me to be with me, wherever I am. Then they will see the glory that you have given me, because you loved me before the world was created.
(John 17:24, CEV)

Jesus prays that we will be with him where he is forever. Here is a word of assurance that provides security for us. We are God's gift to Christ secured by the life of Christ. We are preserved from destruction and brought to life by our faith in Christ. In the final analysis, we will be with Christ in time and eternity, where he is.

How does the assurance about your security affect the way you express your faith while in the world?

_____

_____

_____

_____

_____

_____

_____

_____

_____

Good Father, the people of this world don't know you. But I
know you, and my followers know that you sent me.
(John 17:25, CEV)

Jesus cites a reality with which we are all too familiar. Belief leads
to knowledge that adds immeasurably to life, thus giving our existence an enduring quality. We cheat ourselves out of what we can
have because we do not believe. Doubt causes us to fail to see the
opportunities that are at our door. Indifference causes us to miss
what is accessible to us. Stubbornness causes us to be blind because
we refuse to see.

How have you permitted doubt, indifference, and stubbornness
to keep you from the benefits of belief?

I told them what you are like, and I will tell them even more.
Then the love that you have for me will become part of
them, and I will be one with them. (John 17:26, CEV)

Jesus heightens our awareness of what God is like so that God's
love will fill our hearts. Our life is blended with the life of Christ to
the extent that his identity is revealed through our existence. The
life of Jesus will be so intertwined with our lives that our experiences replicate the life of Christ as the Spirit reproduces in us the
work of Christ.

In what ways is the life and work of Christ reproduced in
your life?

_____

_____

_____

_____

_____

_____

_____

_____

_____

_____

If you had faith as a grain of mustard seed, you might say unto this sycamine tree, be thou plucked up by the root, and be thou planted in the sea; and it should obey you. (Luke 17:6)

Jesus gives an axiom to those who recognize that their faith is inadequate as they request stronger faith. What Jesus says is that all you need is a very little bit to get started. And you need to use it properly. Faith, like a seed, must be planted and nourished so that it can release its life and grow. Take the little faith that you have and nourish it through practice. You will be surprised at what will happen in your life. Real faith, however small, is sufficient to accomplish what seems impossible.

What do you need to do to nourish your faith so that you can grow and strengthen your spiritual life?

_____

_____

_____

_____

_____

_____

_____

_____

Were there not ten cleansed? But where are the nine?
(Luke 17:17)

We lack the sense of indebtedness to be thankful for what we have received. We tend to be unappreciative. Either we take for granted the mercy we receive or we embrace what is given to us in life with an attitude of entitlement. Sometimes we are so mesmerized by the magic of the moment that we neglect to consider the source of our good fortune. Certainly, more have been blessed with the mercy they requested than return to say thanks. Which one are you, the one or the nine?

How do you maintain an attitude of gratitude and avoid the peril of ingratitude?

_____

_____

_____

_____

_____

_____

_____

_____

> *There are not found that returned to give glory to God,*
> *save this stranger.* (Luke 17:18)

Contrast the gratitude and the ingratitude of those who share the same blessing. More are ungrateful than grateful, making ingratitude one of the most common vices. Few are grateful more than ungrateful, making gratitude one of the least common responses. Furthermore, gratitude sometimes comes from those from whom it is least expected, thus becoming something extraordinary rather than ordinary.

In what ways are you grateful for the same blessings for which others express no gratitude?

_____

_____

_____

_____

_____

_____

_____

_____

_____

DECEMBER 12 🌿

Arise, go your way: your faith has made you whole.
(Luke 17:19)

The grateful heart, in thanking God, finds what it needs to begin anew. While the grateful and the ungrateful share the same blessings, those who are grateful receive more than a compassionate response to a desperate plea. The grateful one is distinguished by receiving something more: greater faith to believe for even more.

How do you cultivate the grace of gratitude so that faith can make a difference in your life?

_____

_____

_____

_____

_____

_____

_____

_____

_____

_____

> *The kingdom of God comes not with observation:*
> *Neither shall they say, Lo here! or lo there! for, behold*
> *the kingdom of God is within you.* (Luke 17:20-21)

Sometimes we are so preoccupied with future possibilities that we miss the opportunity of potential in the present moment. We try to peer into the future and get a glimpse of tomorrow only to realize that we cannot second-guess what a day will bring. What we seek is often closer than we realize. If you will look within to find the strength you seek in weakness, you will discover that God is closer than you think.

In what ways have you missed the potential of the present because you were preoccupied with future possibilities?

_____

_____

_____

_____

_____

_____

_____

_____

Remember Lot's wife. (Luke 17:32)

Here is a striking reminder of a story about a person with conflicting affections. We easily get attached to what we are accustomed to, finding it difficult to embrace fully what is ahead. Torn in our devotion, we look back longingly for what we are leaving as we are drawn to where we are going. We are fastened more to yesterday than to today that is leading us to tomorrow. We are prevented from embracing where we are going.

How is your clinging to yesterday preventing you from embracing the benefits of today?

_____

_____

_____

_____

_____

_____

_____

_____

_____

_____

*And shall not God avenge his own elect, which cry day and
night unto him, though he bear long with them?* (Luke 18:7)

Jesus encourages us to pray always so that we do not lose heart,
faint, give up, or give in. We are prone from pressures without and
conflicts within to throw in the towel, call it a day, and quit. Jesus
teaches us that persevering prayer empowers us to keep going. In
prayer we find the confidence to face challenges courageously.

How has persevering prayer strengthened you in a time of need?

> *The Pharisee stood and prayed thus with himself, "God,*
> *I thank you, that I am not as other men are, extortionists,*
> *unjust, adulterers, or even as this publican. I fast twice in the*
> *week, I give tithes of all that I possess." (Luke 18:11-12)*

Prayer is not about comparing ourselves with others so we can boast. Prayer is about acknowledging who God is and how gracious God has been to us. Prayer is not about recognition of our privilege. Prayer is acknowledgement of our blessings in a spirit of humility.

In what ways are you prone to compare yourself with individuals so you can boast to God about your piety?

_____

_____

_____

_____

_____

_____

_____

_____

_____

And the publican, standing afar off, would not lift up so much as his eyes unto heaven, but smote upon his breast, saying "God, be merciful to me a sinner." (Luke 18:13)

Prayer affirms what only God can give: mercy. The truly prayerful person begins with realism about our lack of righteousness. Having an honest opinion about our inadequacies is what keeps us from pretending. With God, no pretense is necessary. Come just as you are, humbly acknowledging your need for what God gives.

How are you prone to neglect recognizing your need to confess your inadequacies?

I tell you, this man went down to his house justified rather than the other: for every one that exalts himself shall be abased; and he that humbles himself shall be exalted. (Luke 18:14)

We delude ourselves when we think more highly of ourselves than we ought. We delude ourselves about others when we diminish them to exalt ourselves. When you are satisfied with yourself, you miss the opportunity to be justified by God.

In what ways does self-righteousness get in the way of the justification God makes available to you?

_____

_____

_____

_____

_____

_____

_____

_____

_____

_____

_____

Suffer little children to come unto me, and forbid them not:
for of such is the kingdom of heaven. (Luke 18:16)

Jesus loves children. He accepts and receives them as a reflection of the kingdom of God. They exemplify the qualities that make for faithful disciples. To be childlike is to be thrilled about the wonder of life, to accept your dependence in life, to be thankful for the privilege of life. These are the ingredients that nurture faith that will carry you through life.

What do you have to do to develop the childlike qualities that will give you a faith to sustain you through life?

_____

_____

_____

_____

_____

_____

_____

_____

*Verily I say unto you, whosoever shall not receive the kingdom
of God as a little child shall in no wise enter therein.*
(Luke 18:17)

Children show forth a universal portrait of trust when they willingly accept what they are given with appreciation. To enter as a
child into what the Lord desires to give us, we must recognize our
dependency on the giver's goodness to bequeath an inheritance we
could never earn. Can you trust like a child the inheritance the
Lord has for you?

What would it take for you to develop childlike trust about the
Lord's inheritance for you?

_____

_____

_____

_____

_____

_____

_____

_____

The Son of man is come to seek and to save
that which was lost. (Luke 19:10)

The Lord has come to those who are meandering in confusion,
sadly disillusioned, groping in darkness, searching for light to lead
them to the source of everlasting life. Unfortunately, some will get
in your way to keep you from getting what the Lord has for you.
Take the initiative to move ahead of whatever or whoever blocks
you from seeing Jesus for yourself. Whatever you encounter—
inaccuracies, inconsideration, or prejudice, whether sacred or sec-
ular—put yourself in a position to see Jesus for yourself.

What do you need to do to get a glimpse of Jesus for yourself?

_____

_____

_____

_____

_____

_____

_____

_____

_____

_____

> *Take heed that you be not deceived: for many shall come*
> *in my name, saying, I am Christ; and the time draws near:*
> *go you not therefore after them.* (Luke 21:8)

Aware that we can be misled, Jesus cautions us to be aware and alert so we may discern between what is real and counterfeit. There are always those who can prey on our uncertainty about the future. While it is natural to want to know about what will be and when, our real focus should always be on fulfilling our purpose in the present. That way we will always be ready whenever the end comes. Our curiosity will never uncover what no one really knows.

In what ways are you susceptible to being deceived by counterfeit faith?

_____

_____

_____

_____

_____

_____

_____

_____

> *But when you shall hear of wars and commotions,*
> *be not terrified: for these things must first come to pass;*
> *but the end is not by and by.* (Luke 21:9)

In focusing on the future, we are admonished to trust in God in the midst of terrifying events. While there will be frightening difficulty—national, international, and natural calamities—we can trust the Spirit to empower us. We have the assurance that God has it all under control and we will trust the Lord through everything.

How can trust in God give confidence and hope when frightening difficulty occurs?

_____

_____

_____

_____

_____

_____

_____

_____

_____

And there shall be signs in the sun, and in the moon, and in the stars; and upon the earth distress of nations, with perplexity; the sea and the waves roaring; People's hearts failing them for fear and for looking after those things which are coming on the earth: for the powers of heaven shall be shaken.
(Luke 21:25-26)

Trust God when your heart fails because of the terror that happens on earth. God will preserve and see you through the worst catastrophes. Calamity is creation's way of preparing for the birth of what is coming, a new age full of glory and majesty. Put your trust in God, then wait and see.

In what ways can you begin to trust God more to keep your heart from failing when disaster is threatening?

*And then shall they see the Son of man coming in a
cloud with power and great joy.* (Luke 21:27)

Something good can come out of something that is utterly devastating. The best can happen even in the worst of circumstances. The Lord appears when all hope is gone and all joy subsides. With an authority peculiar only to the Lord and majesty that no one can duplicate, the Lord surprises us with a great "I gotcha" moment or "I told you so" instance.

How have you been surprised by what the Lord has brought out of something that was horrible for you?

_____

_____

_____

_____

_____

_____

_____

_____

And when these things come to pass, then look up, and lift up your heads; for your redemption draws nigh. (Luke 21:28)

Redemption comes amid ruin as deliverance comes in distress and triumph comes through trial. Lift up your head and look up to see beyond what is happening to what is about to dawn. By looking up, instead of toward the end, you will see a new beginning. Look up to put your mind at ease. See hope. Look up for in that upward gaze you will see relief in Christ.

In what ways can you look up to see the redemption that draws nigh in calamity?

_____

_____

_____

_____

_____

_____

_____

_____

If you can believe, all things are possible to him that believes.
(Mark 9:23)

We question the Lord's ability because it seems that our situation is hopeless. We have tried to do what we know to do only to be disappointed by those we trusted. Jesus makes us aware that the Lord's ability is not the issue. Our faith quotient makes the difference. Faith has unlimited benefits for those who are willing to exercise theirs.

What would it take for you to enlarge your faith quotient so that you could experience the unlimited power that comes with belief?

_____

_____

_____

_____

_____

_____

_____

_____

_____

_____

_____

_____

Do you believe that I am able to do this? (Matthew 9:28)

The Lord wants to know if we believe that he can do what we ask. The key to opening a door we want to enter through is faith to trust and believe. By our response to the Lord, we determine what will happen to make a lasting difference in our life.

How have you circumvented the difference faith would have made in your life?

_____

_____

_____

_____

_____

_____

_____

_____

_____

_____

_____

According to your faith be it unto you. (Matthew 9:29)

Faith is the condition on which we receive favor. Our faith determines so much about our lives: whether we continue attempting to navigate our way on our own accord, knowing full well that we cannot see our way clear, or whether we trust the Lord to answer our plea so that our life can be changed forever.

Would you receive what you request by the way you believe, or would you be denied in your unbelief?

_____

_____

_____

_____

_____

_____

_____

_____

_____

_____

_____

How is it that you do not understand? (Mark 8:21)

It is sad to experience the goodness and generosity of God only to misunderstand God's true intent and meaning in bestowing favor on us. We might just as well not remember what has been done if we are going to misinterpret what it means. We are overwhelmed with anxiety and cares because we fail to understand and remember God's powerful goodness and generosity that we have known and seen. It seems that the Lord can never do enough to convince us of the depth of care and concern God has for us.

In what way have you misunderstood the Lord's goodness and generosity toward you?

_____

_____

_____

_____

_____

_____

_____

_____

_____

_____

And I say to you what I say to all, Watch. (Mark 13:37)

Be alert and vigilant. Do not become slack and negligent—so easy to do as we wait for what we expect. Delay tends to diminish enthusiasm, causing doubt and dissolving excitement. The important thing is not the calendar but our faithfulness. Will you be faithful, found alert, doing what honors God?

How can you keep up your enthusiasm and excitement about being alert and remaining watchful? Does your life honor God?

_____

_____

_____

_____

_____

_____

_____

_____

_____

_____